W.B.Burton
12/25/91

Christmas in My Bones

Christmas in My Bones

W.C. "Mutt" Burton

**Illustrated by
Tim Rickard**

**Compiled by
Anna Morehead Nelson Hunt**

Edited by Erik Bledsoe

Down Home Press, Asheboro, N.C.

Copyright 1991 by W.C. Burton
First Printing, November 1991
Printed in the United States of America

All rights reserved.
No part of this book may be reproduced
by any means without permission of the publisher,
except for brief passages in reviews and articles.

Publisher's Cataloging in Publication
(Prepared by Quality Books Inc.)

Burton, William Clarence, 1907-
    Christmas in my bones / W.C. "Mutt" Burton;
illustrated by Tim Rickard; compiled by Anna
Morehead Nelson Hunt; edited by Erik Bledsoe.
    p. cm.
    ISBN 1-878086-11-1

    1. Christmas–United States.   I. Rickard, Tim. II.
Hunt, Anna Morehead Nelson. III. Bledsoe, Erik,
ed. IV. Title.

GT4986.A1   394.268282
                                  QBI91-1316

Cover design by Tim Rickard
Book design by Elizabeth House

Down Home Press
P.O. Box 4126
Asheboro, N.C. 27204

*For my daughters,
Anna B. and Martha Jane,*

*for my grandchildren,
Anna Morehead (Mo) and Jason,*

and to the memory of Martha.

Preface

There is an old, eloquent, and perhaps naive folk expression which I have not heard much in recent years. People used to say, "I've got Christmas in my bones."

It indicates a feeling which stirs – or should stir – in the human marrow at the approach of and throughout the Christmas season. It is a warm, gentle excitement, a quiet, rejoicing merriment that comes from deep inside and fills the heart and tingles in the blood. It comes from seeing clear winter nights filled with crisp air and brilliant stars, from bright windows in homes and shops, from candles and tinsel and gay packages and children's faces. I've got Christmas in my bones.

Contents

Addicted to Christmas 1
The Truth about Santa Claus 7
Christmas Trees 13
A Dickens of a Christmas 19
The Signs of Christmas 25
Sweeter by the Dozen 29
Sick for Christmas 43
Christmas Magazines 47
Christmas Beard 51
Home for Christmas 55
Christmas Morning 64
A Christmas Story 68
The Days of Christmas 74
Letter to Santa 78
Christmas Fireworks 83
Christmas Greenery 89
The Heart of Christmas 94
Christmas Shopping 99
Christmas Present and Past 104
Mo Christmas 108
The Christmas Feeling 114
Christmas in Old Salem 117
Christmas Memories 122
The Mysteries of Christmas 132

*Christmas gets newer every year
because the Christmas spirit renews
and refreshes the heart.*

– W.C. Burton

Addicted to Christmas

It is well known by everyone to whom I am well known that I am deeply, unremittingly addicted to Christmas. I love all of its signs and symbols. I love the warmth and adornments of the merry time, the legends and lore of the holidays, religious and secular.

All of it still stirs in me the excitement and gladness that I felt about it as a child. I look forward to it with the same eagerness which it has stirred in me since I was just old enough to mispronounce Santa Claus. Its golden mystery has not faded by a fraction of shade or lustre. I never stopped believing in St. Nick because of my maturing suspicions that the Gospel According to Clement Clarke Moore might not be based entirely on scientific fact. For that matter my faith in the legendary Saint and my faith in Mr. Moore remain intact, sturdier than ever. They are part of the

Christmas in My Bones

poetry of Christmas – and if poetry is not real, nothing is.

As I write, we are once more on the threshold of yet another Christmas. I am glad and thankful. True, nowadays I am glad and thankful to be on the threshold of yet another 4th of July, another St. Swithin's Day, Valentine's Day, Ground Hog Day or the anniversary of the invention of the hairpin with the hump. But Christmas always was and is the best.

Christmas is not only a holiday, a symbolic festival of the utmost importance in Christendom. It is many things joyous. It is a most felicitous state of mind and heart and spirit. It is a time of loving and giving, of gathering the family together, of "God rest ye merry, gentlemen" and of buying for the wife things which cost a bit more than ye can afford.

Well, "Tis the season to be merry." Let us greet and keep it with gladness. Christmas has always seemed to me a shining tower at the end of the weary year, a beacon to illuminate its closing and to light the way for the entrance of a brand-new, unused year, forever full of promise and hope. There is a tingle in the crisp air that is unlike any other winter signal. There is a more luminous steel blue in the night sky and a sharper brilliance of stars at Christmas than at any other time of the year.

Fold your checkbook, take your hands off your pocketbook, sit still and listen to your heart – you can feel that tingle. Walk outside on a clear Christmas night and look up at the stars – it is a practice advocated by wise men.

No longer quite a boy, to say the least (and I'm going to say the least about that), I have never become immune to the excitement of Christmas. Every single year I feel the pleasurable sensation. I am stirred by the atmosphere, infused with the warmth, the cheer of every detail of Christmas celebration and symbol. The glow of yellow candlelight. The wreath on the door. The Mazda candles and stars in windows. The special warm quality of lighted church windows and home fires. The carols. The old, quiet chronicle of Bethlehem. The holly. The mistletoe. The good things on the table. Christmas Eve. Christmas Day. And the Twelve Days that follow.

I am moved by Christmas starshine and Christmas sunshine, gleaming, even if coldly on every decorated house, every tree and bush, each winter-waxed limb and twig. I welcome the greeting of friends, by meeting, by mail and by telephone. Of great importance to me is the Christmas tree, bauble-bright with color, a cone of cheer, a beatitude of green bough and brilliance, its gay shower of lights casting magic over a room.

And I like, to be sure, the surprise packages under the tree, more made of generous affection than material matter. One parcel in particular is always there, a bountiful bag of memories, souvenirs of Christmases past, ever increasing, old yet ever new, ever more treasured. Memories of gifts, enjoyed more in the giving. The wooded quest for the elusive, perfect Christmas tree. The Christmas you didn't get as much as you expected and discovered that wasn't the meaning of Christmas. The Christmas you got more than you expected and discovered that, too, was the not meaning of Christmas. Above all, the dear, bright faces, now vanished but held in the heart.

Our Christmases form a chain of jeweled memo-

Christmas in My Bones

ries, to which a new link is added each December. Images forgotten, or half-forgotten, at other times suddenly flicker to bright life in the light of a candle or a Christmas tree, at the sound of a word or a song. Such recollections come to me, as I believe they do to most of us, different ones on different days and hours. Some come many times. Some not brought to life for many years may suddenly come swirling out of the mist again, conjured by a stray connection beyond knowing, a light, a mood, a passing movement, some hidden facet catching a new gleam, lingering or brief as a breath.

One such memory is that of my father, his six-foot frame snugly wrapped in a comfortable overcoat (for he had a strong distaste for cold weather), his back broad and straight as he dragged our Christmas tree from the woods and I walked along behind him. We had searched diligently through acres of woods on a crisp, sunny December day for exactly the right tree, shapely and full, and we found it and bore it home, a cone of evergreen beauty, to be deluged with garlands and tinsel and foil icicles. From this glittering avalanche peeped balls, birds and other baubles of crisply thin glass, many of them preserved carefully from one Christmas until the next for years. Some were slightly worn and chipped, the color of silver and gold finishes a little faded, flaked and soiled, but the more treasured for it. My mother, smiling, granted my gaudy taste in decor.

Our Christmas tree decorations were stored off-season in the attic of my father's neighborhood grocery store. I can remember clearly the excited swelling in my heart when the big cardboard boxes filled with the bright trinkets were brought down. (It is repeated today when I haul our own boxes of decorations from under the eaves of our house.)

There was rarely anything new on our tree in the home place. A few feet of fat new tinsel gleamed there every few years, but the old tarnished threadbare tinsel went on as well. And loads of icicles.

Always there were new foil icicles, loads of them. The tree was drenched with icicles, sparkling in any light. They were especially radiant in firelight. I used to turn out the room lights and build up the coal fire in the grate to see the tree come alive with dancing reflections. I watched it entranced. The decorating, overdone by me, was shiny, not artistic.

Yes, by the frosty beard and jolly belly of Santa Claus, I love it all, including the echoing memory of fireworks thundering in and crackling through the Christmases of my boyhood. It was a custom in the southeast and a few dollars dispatched to the Spencer Fireworks Company out in Ohio would bring you a splendid arsenal of lusty salutes and cherry-bombs with which to detonate the happy days. Most of our fireworks were noisy. I think now that was because we were so jam-packed with the joy of the season that the explosion of a powerful salute (sending a tin can roof high perhaps) was like a shout of glee within us, more forceful, more eloquent than anything else we could muster.

There are thousands of memories of Christmases with Martha, my late wife, and more thousands filled with the bright, sweet faces of our daughters, Martha Jane and Anna B., and in due time with the added rich-

Christmas in My Bones

es of Anna Morehead and Jason, our grandchildren, now grown.

Now, Christmas Day and the Twelve Days to follow are clearly in view. My fresh-cut tree stands in its corner, the handsomest tree that ever graced a mountain slope by consent of witnesses. And beneath it, that bundle of memories.

The Truth about Santa Claus

A wire story urging parents to tell their children there is no Santa Claus came clacking grumpily across the nation a few years back and into the columns of the daily press. It wasn't because AP, UPI, Reuter's or some other wire service was taking a stand against Kris Kringle. The opposition was voiced by a psychologist.

Apparently this Dr. Papp, the psychologist, had got the ear of a desperately copy-hungry wire service correspondent. Dr. Papp, it seems, is dreadfully afraid our children will be warped by the gentle traditional legend. He thinks it destroys a child's confidence in the simon pure honesty of his parents when it dawns upon the developing mind that a fat little man in a red suit couldn't possibly make it down all those chimneys. Not in one night anyway.

Christmas in My Bones

Dr. Papp is of the firm opinion that editor Francis P. Church should have written eight-year-old Virginia O'Hanlon back in 1897 a thundering "No, Virginia, there is no Santa Claus!" and let the *New York Sun* bleat out the noble truth.

I should mention here that "Dr. Papp" was not the real name of the psychologist in the newspaper story – it was simply the name suggested to me by the quality of his utterances to the press. Of course this psychologist is not the first person to have wagged his head dolefully over the jolly fiction. There have been others who took the matter seriously and opposed all forms of fabrication. This, to be sure, is the right of free citizens and they are welcome to it.

It strikes me, however, that Dr. Papp and his kind are a tiresome lot. They have stern souls and set lips. They lay great store by what they regard as reality, not knowing its terribly fragile nature. They seek truth only in science and in a thing they call "fact" – which is the last place they will ever find it. And they do talk such nonsense.

When I was a child I believed in Santa Claus. I still do. There is a difference of conception. That is all. And that is relatively unimportant. I remember distinctly when I believed in Santa literally. Whole cloth. Lock, stock and barrel. Dasher, Dancer, Donder, Blitzen – the works.

I remember, too, when I began to suspect that the North Pole was a pretty remote base for that pre-jet age and that it would be a long, hard haul for "eight tiny reindeer," dragging that sleigh full of toys around through the air with the pilot stopping every whip-

Christmas in My Bones

stitch to pop down a chimney. Then one day I came upon some hard evidence.

Our house was heated by open fireplaces and the dining room remained cold and shut off from the rest of the house during most of the winter. The dining room fire might blaze up with festive warmth for the family Thanksgiving dinner and the Christmas dinner, but, like most people with the same heating system, we ate nearly all our winter meals in the kitchen. There the big wood-burning kitchen range not only prepared our meals and kept them warm, it made us snugly comfortable for their enjoyment.

It was my mother's custom to pile our family Christmas gifts on the long dining room table while it was out of commission for its regular purpose. As the gifts were bought and wrapped and tagged, she placed them on the table in that cold, shut-off room, until they were put on or under the Christmas tree on Christmas Eve. This took place after I had gone to sleep – at least to bed. An unreasonable excitement, a kind of delicious torture of waiting, often kept me wide-eyed in wakefulness long after my parents had gone to sleep.

I knew the gifts were stored in the dining room and I knew that some of them would be for me, though not, as I then thought, the ones from Santa Claus. Obviously they would remain in his shop at the North Pole until he brought them down our chimney. The room was never locked, but there was a tacit understanding that, on my honor, I would not pry.

As an aid to secrecy and the greater security of Christmas surprises, my mother covered the table and the gifts with a large white damask cloth. I can remember the dim winter light of late afternoons in that dining room, the bracing chill and the tingle of wondrous expectancy foreshadowed by the dim shapes under that white cloth.

To this day, an unheated dining room in winter brings a sharp, happy recollection of Christmas to me. I used to slip in now and then just to titillate myself with the unknown pleasures of the approaching Christmas Morning and the general delights of the season.

Then, one day, after I had begun to wonder about that fellow Santa Claus, I was tempted beyond my strength. I lifted the cloth and found among the treasures two or three packages tagged "To William from Santa Claus." Confronted with this evidence, my parents made a clean breast of it and cheerfully admitted that they were, indeed, Santa Claus – as far as my gifts were concerned.

I was not crushed.

I did not feel that my parents were liars who had betrayed my trust and shattered my innocent confidence. Any trace of disenchantment which may have threatened me lasted no longer than five or ten minutes. I was relieved and not in the least cynical. Now there was no nagging doubt. Now the legendary old elf was a brighter figure than ever to me, and merrier. No longer a belief tarnished by suspicion, no longer an image dimmed by "reality," the corpulent, bearded old Saint Nicholas was now revealed to me as the genuinely jolly and generous old gentleman that the secular embodiment of this glowing, sacred season should be.

Christmas in My Bones

I have enjoyed a close friendship with Santa Claus ever since. All the children I ever knew believed in Santa Claus and arrived at much the same sort of exchange, one miracle for another, that came to me. I never knew one of them to go to pieces or to conclude that their parents were no more reliable than a two-dollar bird dog.

Nuts to you, Dr. Papp, but since this is a season of good will to all, I'll make it a bag of mixed Christmas nuts. Santa Claus sends you this message: "Ho, ho hum."

Christmas Trees

The fireplace throws its yellow flamedance across the hearth into the room. The flames murmur and the logs answer with soft crackles. It seems to be a friendly conversation; certainly it is a warm one. The long green needles on a branch of our Christmas tree rest against the right arm of my chair near my elbow, its 140 small bright gleams of color shining among silver loops of tinsel and the customary jewelry. (A pleasant reflection is that all 140 lights burn three watts less than a single 75-watt bulb, and remain cool, adding safety to economy and beauty.)

Granddaughter Anna Morehead, whom we have always called Mo, did the tree decorating job in its entirety. A fine job, too.

The Christmas tree has been a cherished part of my Christmas since my childhood (which was not so many eons ago). When I was a very young child the

Christmas in My Bones

custom of having an ornamented evergreen in the house for the Yuletide was not a prevalent one locally. For most homes in our town it was mainly a matter of holly, maybe a sprig of mistletoe and stockings hung from the mantelpiece. (For a while I was permitted to use a stockingcap on my argument that it qualified under most of its name. It was a piece of headgear of great elasticity and, when unrolled, of uncommon capacity. I felt that it profited me handsomely.)

In those days when few houses had central heating another popular Christmas decoration in the largely rural southeast was running cedar. In the nearby woods it was plentiful. Doors and windows were sometimes outlined with the plant, which suggested living green tinsel. It often festooned mirrors and framed pictures here and there. The heat radius of an open fireplace was not great and running cedar in the home would remain green for several days. It dries quickly and sheds promiscuously in a heated house and nowadays is seldom seen.

Nothing in the way of seasonal decor, however, ever equaled the Christmas tree. And for reasons which remain unclear to me to this day the only tree acceptable for the purpose in these parts was the cedar tree. Its short needles were prickly, making the task of decorating it painful. It began to shed needles almost at once, and it sometimes had a faintly offensive odor. Nevertheless I asked for and got a Christmas tree when I was still very young and I would, for many years, have nothing but a cedar. Tradition. Even so, although I was not an especially daring fellow, I believe I pioneered the pine in our town.

W.C. "Mutt" Burton

There was no commercial traffic in Christmas trees hereabouts in those days.

They did not spring up as temporary forests on street corners and vacant lots. No store sold them. People went walking in woods never far away, felled and bore home a reasonably shapely cedar after a period of frustration during which all cedar trees looked perfect at 30 paces and miserable up close. I have hunted cedars and later pines in woods until I had the eerie feeling that the perfect, full, richly green and symmetrical trees of appropriate size were actually and deliberately showing themselves at a distance and then scurrying off to hide from me, giggling, until they appeared at another spot in the woods, luring me on through a weary zigzagging search of the territory.

On occasion, and usually on request, a farmer might bring a tree or two to town. I had three farmer uncles living in the Monroeton section, eight or 10 miles southwest of my hometown, Reidsville, North Carolina, and my father dealt with many farmer friends at his grocery store. One of them was the bearer of our first Christmas tree. Our tree decorations, which were not expensive, were bought and never discarded, though a new piece or two might be added from time to time. If some of the items grew a little shabby and worn I treasured them more. They were familiar symbols saying we were preparing for that splendid season again.

A cautious man by nature, my father did not permit the use of electric lights on our tree. (A lighted tree, in fact, was fairly rare in any home known to my childhood.) We had glass trinkets, balls and birds and angels to hang on the limbs, and tinsel and red and

W.C. "Mutt" Burton

green garlands of something like plasticized paper crinkles and foil icicles. I still have some of the old pieces in a box marked "Auld Lang Syne." I plan to use them again. Someday. Maybe. Some of them are more than 80 years old, genuine antiques.

When I grew old enough to be entrusted with the trimming of the tree, I seized upon the task and made the most of it. I drenched the tree with foil, glass and garlands. With enthusiasm, I hurled the foil icicles in abundance at its limbs. I have photographs which reveal that my decorating showed more haste than taste, but I thought it a thing of hypnotic beauty.

I am, as I write this, basking in the soft gleam of our fresh-from-the-mountains Christmas tree, the prettiest one ever, it seems to me, although I am aware that I say that – and truly believe it – every year.

For many years we obtained our trees from friend and neighbor Howard Briggs, who had Christmas tree farms in the Virginia mountains. No one tended them better or brought them fresher to town. While employed at the Reidsville branch of the American Tobacco Co., Howard, who loves to grow things, developed a highly successful nursery and operated it on the side. In 1970 he retired from American Tobacco Co. and retained only Christmas trees as nursery stock.

At one time, there were three Howard Briggs Christmas Tree Farms in Floyd County, Virginia, all on the West Branch of Little River. He tended his trees lovingly all year, harvested several thousand annually, most of which he sold at wholesale, but he always brought a select few home for local sale to friends and

Christmas in My Bones

others who appreciated the best in the tannenbaum line.

After we married, Martha did the decorating of our tree, with my full consent. Then our daughters took it over. Now the decorating is done by my granddaughter, Mo. But the tree at my elbow is as enchanting to me as the ones that glistened in the firelight of my boyhood home. The decorating, of course, is far superior.

A Dickens of a Christmas

Of the many writers who have written of Christmas, none has done so with heartier feeling and more personal enthusiasm than Charles Dickens. Although numerous Yule pieces flowed from his pen – he used to turn out a highly popular Christmas annual – his *A Christmas Carol* has become a set piece, as much a symbol and part of Christmas as holly, a lighted tree, stockings by the fire, or Santa Claus himself.

The reading of *A Christmas Carol* is a standard ritual in many homes. Public readings and dramatizations of the story are steadily recurring productions on radio, television and in auditoriums and church basements all over the English speaking world. The ultimate, exhaustive benediction of Tiny Tim is also, I daresay, uttered to farther-flung gatherings, in multiple translations.

Christmas in My Bones

It is even said that Charles Dickens, unquestionably the best known and best loved of all writers of Christmas stories, came to believe that Christmas belonged to him, that he invented it and it was his personal property. This was a carping jest for Dickens obviously rejoiced in the sentiment that Christmas belongs to everyone – forever. He was pleased to comment upon the season in redolent prose that crackles with the cheeriness and warmth of an open fire. In a certain sense, however, that piece of literary levity is not so wide of the mark. If Dickens did not actually invent Christmas and own it, he contributed to its lay concept and celebration more lavishly than all other writers on the subject put together and bound with red ribbon and a garland of holly.

There is adequate record that Christmas was far more than literary fodder to the creator of Fezziwigs. In the bosom of the Dickens family, the Yuletide was celebrated with gusto and genuine enthusiasm. The house was lush with Christmas greenery, bright with color, candlelit and filled with all of the feeling and atmosphere that Dickens put on paper. Dickens worked himself into a fine, bubbly lather over the open-handed good cheer. There were pantomimes which Dickens composed, directed and produced in his home that turned the house into a Christmas theater and the place is said to have brimmed with jollity and heart-felt laughter. Being an actor of ardor and considerable skill he frequently appeared in such productions as well.

Congenial friends came in a constant stream to share the Dickens cheer, to join in the family caroling,

Christmas in My Bones

to light candles and poke the log and feast on the special goodies and quaff from a warming cup. They came, too, for what was even more important, to bask in the bright spirit of a man who had both a reverent and ebullient feeling for Christmas and all that it stood for – and still stands for. Throughout the season the Dickens home was the bailiwick of open-hearted, caring friendship where people could be sheltered by a roof under which the joy of the season shone like a lamp. Nor did the happy revels cease until the full Twelve Days of Christmas were spent and well spent.

The biographers of Charles Dickens tell us that at Christmas time he was a boy again, a merry, happy boy, a condition denied him in its proper chronological order. He forgot the cold, harsh times of his youth. He abandoned all the disappointments, all the pain and struggle and bitterness which had on occasions been thrust upon him. His spirits were revived and they sang in a renewed faith in God and man, just as the heartily simple, ardently sentimental story of *A Christmas Carol* sings his belief in the redemption of a miserly curmudgeon through a terrifying revelation of his meanness combined with the pervading Christian charity and human kindness of Christmas.

If anyone should regard such a love for and delight in Christmas as naive, let him be assured, and right gladly, that it is so. And let him look to the roots of that word. The season is in observance of the Nativity. It is the celebration of a Child. It is the time of greatest hope and promise and shining faith. It is thus the naive shall inherit the earth.

I believe it is safe to say (and safe or not I'll say it)

that Charles Dickens was the most remarkable popular writer who ever lived. It is true that he lived at a time when the confector of printed tales had no such competition as that with which the modern and especially the electronic age has supplied us – I will not say blessed us.

His books usually appeared first in serial form, often in one of the widely circulated periodicals of the day. Considering the rather sparsely settled state of America in Dickens' day compared to the hustling, noisy, congested throngs that populate it today, the hail and hurrah that greeted Dickens at the dock of New York on his later visit to this country made the lustiest to-do that ever greeted the Beatles seem almost a show of indifference.

Thousands of readers of *The Old Curiosity Shop* are said to have met a ship bearing the author to these shores in advance of certain chapters which were expected to disclose Nell Trent's state of health, known to be parlous at last reports. Nell Trent was the heroine of *The Old Curiosity Shop* and was known far better to Dickens' following as "Little Nell." At sight of Dickens the throng cried out in anguished unison, "Does Little Nell die?" She did and readers wept openly.

In Dickens' day the writing and publishing of Christmas stories and publications was almost a major, if seasonal, industry. "Christmas Annuals" poured from the presses, and those which carried stories by Dickens were seized while the ink was still moist.

I have treasured copies of *The London Illustrated News, Punch, The Sphere* and *The Spectator* from the

Christmas in My Bones

1930s and early 40s which still reflected these annuals in their "Special Christmas Editions," full of fancy, romantic colored illustrations, sentimental tales and mellow humor in tribute to the Yuletide.

It is hard to believe that there is anyone over the age of three (and few under that) who do not know of the enduring existence of Ebenezer Scrooge and Tiny Tim. The story of their long-ago Christmas is read and reread privately and publicly each year. It is also projected on our TV screens with unfailing regularity, sometimes in aborted form. Why do they keep hacking out these new and almost invariably inferior shadows of the wonderfully syrupy old chronicle? (And what in the name of Vermont is wrong with syrup?)

There is a very decent American movie with (as I recall) Lionel Barrymore as Scrooge. And there is a superb English film of Dickens' *A Christmas Carol* with Alastair Sim as the most perfect Scrooge ever and a production of excellence not likely to be equaled by the TV journeymen. I have seen it on TV once or twice, so it is surely available. I'd welcome it and watch it with pleasure flavored by traditional tears.

Dickens, with help from some of our early scribes, notably Washington Irving, but Dickens far more than anyone else, shaped our sentiments and celebration of Christmas. He brought the Christmas Story to more people than anyone excepting Saints Matthew, Mark, Luke and John, the great chroniclers of the First Christmas. With no thought of canonizing Charles Dickens I think the four Saints might look upon his secular treatment with some favor.

The Signs of Christmas

Do you know what the signs of Christmas are?
I think I know
For I have been a Christmas watcher all my years,
Loving the joyous, luminous season all my life,
More now than yesteryear or yesterday,
More now than ever.

Are not the advertising signs, the bright warm colors
And familiar images in magazines,
On TV screen and billboards on the highways,
Or in store windows, saying what a grand
Gift this gimmick, that gimcrack or gadget
Or such-and-such a thingamabob would make
For father, mother, sister, baby brother,
Sweetheart, grandma, favorite uncle, aunt
Or whomever.
Not that I am against these things. No sir.

Christmas in My Bones

Christmas is commercialized, you say?
And so it is, but look at it this way,
They do brighten the sight a bit,
Those flossily decorated, ribbon-wrapped,
Spangle-adorned and cheerily embellished
Articles for sale as gifts
(You can wait till after Christmas to pay.)
And another thing
Maybe, just maybe, there'll be a kind of feedback,
So that the pure Christmas spirit
Will work its way into the commercialization.
Well, Heaven knows a little purity of spirit
Would greatly improve our commerce.

Nor are the bonafide, genuine signs,
The things of home,
The candlelight aura, the warm bronzing
Orbit of the fireside, the close affection
Of the hearth and heart
At Christmas Time.
The jeweled glitter of the Christmas tree,
The silver-shine against the dark woods green,
With the promise of bundled, secret treasures
Piled there for Christmas dawn's discovery,
These are not the signs.
Nor family nor faithful friends nor feasting.
Not even the bright, wondering faces of little children
Are the signals, as many so long have said,
For these are reflections of the season
That is the lovely marvel of the year.
Though all these things I list I fondly hold,
Deeply dear within my mind and heart,
They are not, I think and say, the signs.

W.C. "Mutt" Burton

The signs of Christmas, wondrous, singing signs,
Are in the air and in the light,
Are on the earth, across the sky.
The blue sky of a clear day in this season
Is not merely fair or cerulean blue
But a Christmas blue.
And clouds upon a cloudy day
Have more silver far than gray.
All days of this very special time
Are lit with very special glistening,
And the air has a very special tingle.
Look closely at the distant trees.
They are not bare and blackened bones,
But etchings on a sheet of light,
A lovely, lacy frieze of earth and sky,
While nearer trees seem softly gilded.
Observe the night for in some ways
The nights shine brighter than the days,
With stars in crystal cobalt black,
Afire in black sapphire,
So dazzling closely bright they seem to make
A sound like anthems, curls in the sky.
While earthly carols, old sweet sounds,
Are sweeter still because of being borne
On air that's crisply charged with mystery.

Now you may say these are imagined things,
Knowing it is Christmas Time, expectation,
The colors of custom touching
All these signs I see.
Or you may say it is the way they are
This time of year, in winter,

Christmas in My Bones

The light, the air, the earth, the sky,
The way the sun slants or the stars sing out.
(It is true, the stars have told this story
Since that First Day in Bethlehem.)

But if you'll look, will really look,
I think you'll see, will truly see,
All that I say of day and night,
Of earth and sky and stars and light
Is true at Christmas Time.

Sweeter by the Dozen

Let Christmas begin on December 26th, for that is the day it should begin. And the greeting, the wish, merry Christmas, should regain its original meaning, not necessarily the connotation that it has acquired over the centuries.

I shall, as you might have guessed, explain.

The proper Christmas celebrant has two periods and two ways of enjoyment. First there is the excitement, the tingle of looking forward to Christmas; the business of making the home a bright bower for the festival, the arrangement of happy surprises for Christmas Morning. Then there are the twelve days that follow and which should be and can be the best of all.

The day after Christmas Day is the first of the Twelve Days of Christmas, contrary to a fairly common assumption. December 26 represents the day the

Christmas in My Bones

Magi began their 12-day journey to the manger in Bethlehem, following the appearance of a guiding star in the east.

You will observe that I did not say the day after Christmas, but the "day after Christmas Day." There is all the difference in the world. Christmas is just beginning.

This is based on ancient Yuletide tradition in England and in certain countries on the European continent. So, by ancient tradition – and you just can't find a better type of tradition than that – the Twelve Days of Christmas begin the day after Christmas Day and continue through January 6, known as Twelfth Night and marked by the celebration of Epiphany or the Feast of Lights.

On December 26, the days approaching Christmas, days that drag by in laggardly ticking hours for youngsters and hurrying, scurrying hours for grownups, are now past. The preparation, the decorating, the cooking and baking, the frantic, often frustrating, always expensive shopping, have been done. Gifts have been distributed and only some paying-for remains. Now is the time to collect the true dividends of all that to-do.

Now is the time to look, to really look, at the glowing tree. In the past few days you have seen it only as one glimpses the blur of traffic lights in passing. Sit quietly and see it now. Regard its silent shimmer. Note the way that amber bulb casts a warm haze of light on the wall. Observe how the silver ball on that long limb is reflected from the picture nearby and how the foil icicles toss mysterious flickers against the ceiling.

Now is the time to sit with your family in your

W.C. "Mutt" Burton

Christmas home, to talk with old friends and read the new books and magazines, to browse in Christmas. Now is the time to take Christmas up and taste it slowly, to breathe its bouquet as a gentle wine.

That's where the original meaning of "merry Christmas" comes in. Father Francis X. Weiser, S.J., of Weston College in Weston, Massachusetts, a Christmas scholar, makes this particular point in his informative little volume called *The Christmas Book*.

"When this greeting was originally used, the word 'merry' did not mean 'joyful, hilarious, gay,' as it does today. In those days it meant 'blessed, peaceful, pleasant,' expressing spiritual joys rather than earthly happiness. It was thus used in the famous phrase, 'Merry England.'

"The well-known carol, 'God rest you (sic) merry, gentlemen,' is an excellent example of the original meaning of 'merry.' The position of the comma clearly shows the true meaning (that the word is not an adjective describing 'gentlemen') and therefore is not 'God rest you, joyful gentlemen,' but 'God rest you peacefully, gentlemen.' " Thus spake Weiser.

The *Oxford English Dictionary* takes more than a page to give "merry" a good working over and repeatedly defines it as meaning "pleasant," "agreeable" and on occasion, "favorable" as in the old nautical term, "a merry wind." The OED says the word had no reference to hilarity, mirth-provoking or merry-making until a "modern" sense conveyed such meanings.

Webster's Unabridged, Second Edition, adds the definition, "savory," noting, however, that this use is archaic. Archaic or not, I like it. I think it is my favorite

Christmas in My Bones

definition, especially as applied to Christmas. For Christmas should be savored. And now – and throughout the Twelve Days – is the time to do it.

Savor Christmas. Taste it. Roll it around on your tongue, so to speak. And in your mind. And in your memory. And, best of all, in your heart.

Take time to observe Christmas, not with any formal sort of celebration necessarily, but within yourself, quietly, privately, but keeping a communion of warmth and love with your family and friends. Read and rest with the cheering glow of candles and Christmas tree nearby. If it is possible, include in that arrangement an open fire. A wood fire is best, with the logs murmuring their serene benediction and flavoring the room with a gentle incense.

"Let's look at one another," cries Emily, desperate in a sudden awareness, too late, of hasty existence in Thornton Wilder's play, *Our Town*. "Touch hands, touch hands," is a poet's Christmas plea. They are urgent needs of the human heart, filled with fresh pertinence at Christmas time. Let us take time to look at one another – to touch hands. And to look long and lovingly, at Christmas itself.

I have always been saddened by the sheer wastefulness of sweeping Christmas out with the torn tissue and raveled ribbons on the very day after Christmas Day – on the very day that the truly merry Christmas should begin. After all the fever and labor of making ready for the wonderful and glowing season, too many people simply snip it off and toss it out before it has really begun, thereby cheating themselves of its beauty and blessings.

W.C. "Mutt" Burton

They have paid and prepared for a feast, have seated themselves tentatively at the table, have tasted a mere morsel of the first course and waved the rest away. They starve their souls and leave their spirits famished, their hearts hungry.

Many years ago my friend Holley Mack Bell, a sensitive, sensible man who was at the time the associate editor of the *Greensboro Daily News*, and I found ourselves in ardent agreement on the full celebration of the Christmas season. Holley Mack professed to suffering pain to a point pretty near excruciating at the very thought of such thoughtless waste. I felt somewhat likewise. So we got together and we formed the World Wide Twelfth Night Society (WWTNS) formerly World Wide Order of Twelfthnighters (WWOoT).

With what might be called a benevolent seizure of power, I named Holley Mack permanent president of the WWTNS (or WWOoT, as it was known then). It so happens that I was his campaign manager. To begin with I was the chairman of the nominating committee. In point of fact I was also the sole election official and the solitary voter, but since my vote was heartily in favor of Holley Mack, he is, as I see it, not only legally but unanimously elected. There were no other candidates visible in the field. I merely took advantage of a monotonous absence of contention for the title and bestowed it on Holley Mack. He has no duties or privileges greater than any other member. I felt that even so unorganized an organization as the WWTNS should have a president.

We are loosely but, I hope, effectively organized.

Christmas in My Bones

We invite all and sundry to become members and there are no initiation fees, no difficult rituals and no dues. There is no roll call, in fact no recorded roster. If you observe the Twelve Days of Christmas in a cheerful, quiet, well-behaved manner you are automatically enrolled. Of course we don't know how many members we have, but we are hopeful. We hope there are many and we hope they are faithfully following the tenets of our society, which are precious few and easily followed if you get in the right frame of mind. We operate on the honor system.

The Twelfth Night Society has no meeting schedule – in truth no meetings in the way most organizations have. Whenever two friends, two people of good will and like mind on the subject of the Twelve Days of Christmas, meet, that we declare to be an official meeting of WWTNS. Whoever they are, whenever and wherever they meet, they are a quorum.

In case you are wondering about the change of the organization's name, let me explain. There was nothing wrong with the World Wide Order of Twelfthnighters in full, but the initials spelled out a sort of word that came to seem just a trifle brusk, even somewhat belligerent and thus counter in expression to the nature of the organization. WWOoT was not refined enough for WWTNS.

The change of name came about recently, just a few minutes ago in fact. The motion was made and carried by a unanimous vote of all the members present, which happened to be me. I am sure, however, that President Bell would have sent me his proxy if he had known the matter was going to come up.

W.C. "Mutt" Burton

Perhaps it is true that World Wide Twelfth Night Society is a rather pretentious title since WWTNS has no actual organizational structure, no fees, no funds, no meetings. It doesn't even have any committees, which I hold to be one of its sterling qualities. The title is justified in simple truth, however. There are people in all parts of the world who unfailingly observe the full Twelve Days and we are certainly associated in spirit, which is quite enough.

The credo, the rules and bylaws of the Twelfth Night Society are all as simple as day – or as simple as the Twelve Days – and are rolled into one grand plan. We believe in observing the full Christmas season. We point out to all who will hear that the Christmas season begins on Christmas Eve and continues until Epiphany, sometimes called Old Christmas, January 6.

In this way the true celebrant gets a sort of bonus of two extra days since this runs to 14 days, but that's all right. The 12-day count begins, of course, on the day after Christmas Day – when the wise men saw the star and began their journey to Bethlehem.

The Feast of Epiphany is the Night of the Magi, the night symbolic of that night almost 20 centuries ago when the Wise Men, following the star in the east, found the child.

"And when they were come into the house, they saw the young child with Mary his mother and fell down, and worshipped him and when they had opened their treasures, they presented unto him gifts; gold, and frankincense and myrrh."

How familiar and clear are the words of St. Matthew. How ageless and dear is the story in the

Christmas in My Bones

hearts of the Christian world. And how far, it seems to me, from the real poetry and mysticism and bright beauty given to the world in this birth some of the cant talkers and doctrine makers have dragged the life gift called Christianity. What a drab and dry-bone police state some have made of it.

If I understand anything at all about the Christian spirit, as I conceive it to be in its true form, then Christmas best expresses it. Christmas with all of its color and gaiety, warmth and affection, charity and jollity, yes, including tinsel, Christmas trees, and Santa Claus – all these are a part of a truly good way. This, I feel, should be the complexion of the Christmas spirit all the year round. The holiday trappings, wonderful in their proper place, are not necessary to the general practices of the spirit.

For this good and sufficient reason the Twelve Days of Christmas are also symbolic of the twelve months of the year in my mind.

It has been my custom, annually, to remind the public of the great objective of WWTNS (and of WWOoT when it was that). These reminders have been issued regularly over most of the past three decades. Once, years ago, a column I wrote on the subject jangled the nerves of an inky compatriot on the Southern Pines *Pilot*. He wrote a responding editorial in which he said, in effect, Heavens to Betsy! Perish the thought! He used more words than that, but that's what it amounted to.

Well, now, you see that fellow, a nice man, a bright man, just wasn't thinking clearly. He envisioned 12 days of frantic running about, hectic chores done in a frenzy or maybe a tizzy. He missed the point altogether. I say perish the thought, too. It should be made clear that neither Holley Mack, nor I, nor any true Twelfth-nighter endorses – or even contemplates – the continuation of the frantic and strenuous aspects of Christmas for a dozen added days. Far from it. Indeed just the opposite is true. We advocate the Twelve Days as a relaxed time, a stay-at-home time or quietly-visit-your-friends time. It may contain parties, none if you like none.

Above all it is a time to think and feel and savor and soak up Christmas. It is a season for good books, good talk, good recollections and quiet happiness. It is a family time and a time for all men, women and children. It is a time for deep and sweet awareness. A time to take the time.

The plain, perfectly clear, important and emphatic fact is Christmas lasts twelve days. And this does not even include Christmas Day, which has come to be the highlight of the season, its most festive day. It is, sad to say, the last day of Christmas for all too many. It is rightly an important day, but the Twelve Days follow. They symbolize, as you probably know, even if you do not observe the span, the twelve-days journey of the three wise men following the star to the hallowed manger. Even before there was such a thing as Christmas, when Santa Claus was just an unemployed old gentleman in a red suit, the Twelve Days were feast days. They celebrated the ancient pagan festival of the winter solstice, when Woden, his wife and several other congenial gods and good spirits held their annual procession.

Christmas in My Bones

The full observance has been a more general custom in England than in America. In Great Britain the Christmas season once was filled with traditional observances. There was, of course, the joy of Christmas Day. Then on December 26, the first day of Christmas, there was Boxing Day (having nothing to do with fisticuffs) when servants and menials generally were given money or other rewards in "Christmas boxes." The 27th or second day was St. John's Day, celebrated in places by the blessing and consumption of wine. The third day was Childermas, observed in memory of Herod's "massacre of the innocents."

The fourth day was variously celebrated with the Feast of Fools, a merry mockery of worldly rank, Boys' Feast, when choir boys were richly fed, and more soberly as a time of memorial to the martyred Thomas à Becket. The fifth day had no church connection, but was made entertaining by the telling of traditional ghost stories.

The sixth day was New Year's Eve, followed by New Year's Day, two festive days in their own right, and thus they are integral parts of the Twelve Days. (In Greece the children sang carols to honor St. Basil, who died on January 1, in the year 379.)

The eighth, ninth and 10th days were filled with parties, ballad singing and magic lantern shows. (TV, I suppose, is our modern magic lantern, although not always merrily so.)

There were also Frost Fairs on the frozen Thames River, skating, pantomimes and masques throughout the season. The 11th day, the Eve of Epiphany and the 12th day, Epiphany, celebrating the arrival of the Magi and the manifestation to them of the Christchild, bring Christmas to its only rightful close.

It is regrettable that the all-out celebration of Twelfth Day and Twelfth Night has fallen so sadly into disuse. Only about a century ago it was a thriving observance, with feasting and gifting and games, and playlets and pantomimes and I don't know what-all.

James Henry Leigh Hunt, the English poet, journalist and political liberal (he went to prison for two years because of his journalistic attacks on King George IV) who lived from 1784 until 1859, wrote of the celebration thus:

"Christmas goes out in fine style with Twelfth Night. It is a finish worthy of the time. Christmas Day was the morning of the season; New Year's Day the middle of it or noon; Twelfth Night is the night, brilliant with the innumerable planets of Twelfth-cakes.

"The whole island keeps court; nay, all Christendom. All the world are kings and queens. Everybody is somebody else; and learns at once to laugh at, and to tolerate, characters different from his own by enacting them. Cakes, characters, forfelts, lights, theatres, merry rooms, little holiday-faces, and, last but not least, the painted sugar on the cakes, so bad to eat but so fine to look at, useful because it is perfectly useless except for a sight and a moral – all conspires to throw a giddy splendour over the last night of the season ...."

Mr. Hunt, who employed only the last two of his names as his by-line, was a man after my own heart, wise in a merry way and merry in a wise way. He instantly conjures up with his words a way of life and an outlook in the matter of enjoying a Christmas which

Christmas in My Bones

shows considerable improvement over our too-often weary, hasty and lackadaisical celebration of the season.

It is interesting and pertinent to note that the eyewitness account of the jolly and varied doings set down by Leigh Hunt was written by a man who died four years after our Civil War ended. In so short a time we have lost this immeasurably valuable social and spiritual observance.

Some may be amazed that the people of a mere one hundred years ago – less than the span of some lifetimes – could enjoy themselves so deeply, fully, whole-heartedly, since they did not have automobiles, electric lights, central heating, deep freezer chests, movies, radio, television or even that primitive pioneer of canned home entertainment, the phonograph. Well, they didn't have an energy crisis either. Of any kind.

In the heyday of public and private celebration of the Twelve Days of Christmas there were particular games, customs and rituals for each day and each day was celebrated wholly. If this seems excessive to some, let them be reminded that many people, another English poet, Robert Herrick, among them, believed the time for removing the Yuletide evergreens and decorations, officially ending the season, was Candlemas, February 2, traditionally celebrated by the lighting of many candles. The power of winter's cold and darkness is diminishing and the light from the glowing candles helps speed the departing demons.

That date has been reduced, regrettably, to association with a small rodent known as a groundhog, along with attendant folk superstitions regarding the weather.

One couple of my acquaintance, two of the brightest spirits I have known, Albert and Gladys Coates of Chapel Hill, kept their hospitable home cherry and attractive with Christmas decorations until February 2. And if they ran over that a few days it didn't bother them. They and all their friends got a lot of pleasure from this practice. When "Miss Gladys" gets the house all decorated (using their prettiest Christmas cards of all years mounted as wall hangings), it is too pretty to remove in a couple of weeks.

The World Wide Twelfth Night Society approves of such Yuletide ardor, but will settle for Christmas Eve, Christmas Day and the Twelve Days of Christmas.

I know there are many who, in the interest of caution and safety, urge the prompt disposal of Christmas trees and other seasonal cut greenery, for fear of fire. Editorial urgings appear in the papers and on television. I hope no one will risk or lose anything from such mishaps, but I believe there is a safe way to keep the tree aglow until Epiphany, the Feast of Lights.

Be careful with that feast. Use caution with candles – keep things clear of them. Keep your tree watered before and after decorating it. Use cool lights. Don't bring your tree in the house too early. If the needles get too dry keep the lights turned off and enjoy the reflected light on the baubles.

To some it may seem that the program of the World Wide Twelfth Night Society is a little limited, devoted wholly to a relatively short period of the year. True,

Christmas in My Bones

our prime aim is the full enjoyment and observance of Christmas. I should like to say at this time, however, that we carry on a highly attractive year-long program in an unobtrusive way.

We also encourage celebration of Easter, St. Valentine's Day, the 4th of July, Labor Day, Thanksgiving Day, St. Swithin's Day and the vernal equinox. We advocate candlelight and wine, firelight and friends and moonlight and romance if circumstances permit. We have come out unequivocally for fresh snowfall, spring showers, autumn dusks and summer nights. We place our seal of approval on a wide variety of articles and institutions including good pictures, good reading. sweet repose, the laughter of children, sunsets, Bertie County ham, pretty girls, democracy, the sanctity of the home, turtle watching and time-and-a-half for overtime.

Won't you join us?

Sick for Christmas

I suppose it was the flu. Whatever it was, it was very uncomfortable and extremely inconvenient. It slugged me hard on the morning of Christmas Eve. I am unable to give an accurate clinical diagnosis because I refuse to watch the Lifetime Network on TV and I have been neglecting the *Reader's Digest* recently.

Reporting merely as a layman and victim, I would say that it was the unfair or foul-blow type of flu: the kind that hits below the belt.

I resisted it bravely throughout Christmas Eve and went on valiantly annoying as many clerks and shopkeepers as possible with my late shopping. That evening I wrapped, tagged and deposited my parcels beneath the tree with somewhat less zest and artistry than is customary, left a note for Santa Claus, asking

Christmas in My Bones

him to leave an extra bottle of aspirin tablets in my stocking, and went to bed.

I was double-pooped, triple-bushed and I suffered the odd illusion that my bones had turned to tallow. Nevertheless, I still felt that I would be in fairly normal condition the next day, though I might have to go a little easy on the turkey dressing.

Next morning I arose fairly early – though not without relentless prodding from family – ignited the Yule log and managed a reasonably convincing "Ho, ho, ho" attitude. After the happy ritual of passing out the gifts found in profusion under the bedizened pine, after the bright wrappings were disheveled and the surprises unveiled, I surrendered.

I had planned to spend Christmas Day in the rather pleasant stupor which has become a personal tradition of the season with me – a stupor compounded of fatigue, the relief of merry missions accomplished and the ability to look around, relax and appreciate what all the excitement has been about.

Well, I achieved the stupor all right, but it was not the gentle sort that I enjoy. It was rather a clammy fog. I retreated to the sheets and stretched out with a sigh long enough to reach from Christmas Day to Epiphany. Much of the time was given over to healing sleep, which was not without its compensations.

Now and again visitors popped into the door to wish me a speedy recovery. To this sentiment I responded with deeply felt but feebly expressed appreciation. Some of them asked, "How do you feel?" I could reply to that in graphic particulars. Others asked, "What are you doing getting sick on Christmas Day?"

Christmas in My Bones

I was unable to think of a suitable and polite answer to that one.

I ventured out briefly in mid-Christmas Week, but any appreciable amount of activity seemed to sap my strength. This did not alarm me greatly since sapping my strength has always been a comparatively easy task. However, I looked eagerly forward to having my normal energies, such as they are, restored.

Much of the time of my Yuletide indisposition was spent with my face turned languidly toward the television screen. I became on relatively familiar terms with the weird characters who inhabit the daytime soap operas on TV and the even more eerie lot who appear on game shows. It is, perhaps, a consolation to consider that, were my ailments thrice compounded with beri-beri, they would be nothing compared with the monumental miseries of the shadowy, soapy gnomes; the ghoulish pity and fatuous glee of the impresarios.

After a few days abed, only occasionally did I get the sensation that I had eaten cockleburs. I missed the feasting, the wedges of white meat, the rich stuffings, the luscious gravy, sauces and cake. I retained hope that I would be able yet to pounce upon the carcass of that expensive bird in the refrigerator, garnish it with all the goodies prepared for assaulting the digestive tracts of men of good will, and come up smiling.

I faced the New Year, meanwhile, with that vast and various store of fine, firm resolutions which a man can summon confidently during periods of enforced idleness. It was the first time in my life that I ever spent Christmas Day ill abed. On the whole I do not recommend it.

Christmas Magazines

I dream wistfully of the Christmas when I shall have all my gifts bought and wrapped and my cards mailed some two weeks before Christmas Eve. In this dream the house is decorated and tidy by December 20th, and I am seated, with my family, in front of a cheery fire. I am taking leisurely puffs at a pipe between passages of Dickens. Or I am thumbing through some well-worn Christmas editions of *Punch, The Tattler, The Sphere* and *The Illustrated London News*.

Some years ago I made it an annual habit to buy the Christmas issues of these and other English publications. It was the custom of their publishers then – and may be now for all I know – to produce beautifully elaborate issues at this season, filled with color, illuminated Yuletide rhymes, romantic and sometimes

Christmas in My Bones

swashbuckling adventure tales and a variety of other editorial caprices which filled them with the ruddy atmosphere of Merrie Christmas in Merrie England.

I still have those I bought upward of 60 years ago. Most of the year they are wrapped in dry-cleaner's plastic and tucked away under the eaves along with the Christmas tree decorations and the Moravian stars. But at Christmas time they are taken out, unwrapped and placed on the coffee table in company with current publications, than which they are much more inviting. They have become seasonal set pieces. Every year I put them handily near my easy chair. Every Twelfth Night I put them back in storage with the tinsel, the glass balls, the tree lights and the left-over wrapping paper. I've never got around to reading them, but I keep on hoping that I will.

They are showing some wear, but that only enhances them. With reasonable care they appear able to endure another 60 years and more. They are a part of the Christmas tradition in our house and their sprightly covers and warmly nostalgic, happily innocent contents brighten the place and us each Christmas. I have seen some evidence that British magazines have fared better than those which have survived in America, but I tend to doubt that there is anything quite like these old copies of mine being published today.

At the time I bought them they were priced in the book stores from 75 cents to $1.50 per copy. It was more than a bargain; it was an investment.

In those days, too, chiefly the '30s, I purchased each year the Christmas edition of a French publica-

W.C. "Mutt" Burton

tion called *L'Illustration*. The price, printed on the cover, ranged from 25 francs in 1933 to 35 francs in 1938. The price in American book stores ranged from $2.50 to $3.50. I confess I have not investigated the present market on such matters, but I doubt that there is anything remotely like it – including *L'Illustration* itself, if it is still in existence – being printed in the magazine market today.

The Noel issues of *L'Illustration* achieved an elegance, richness and splendor of craftsmanship far above even the finest practices in the periodical trade elsewhere. It was published at 13 Rue Saint-Georges, Paris, and looked it. The Christmas issues were souvenir items, large and generous. They measured 11 1/4 by 15 inches, were often nearly half-an-inch thick and weighed an average of two-and-one-half pounds. That is, of course, a gross description unworthy of such artistry in the printer's trade as *L'Illustration* represented.

Its layout was exquisite, the precision of its printing, in color and in black-and-white, was unsurpassed. The paper stock on which it was printed was varied in each issue according to the page or section content and was of the finest quality. Its advertising pages were examples of sophisticated imagination and high style.

The art work was superb. I have seen nothing like it to this day, even in the finest and most expensive art books. If there was a section dealing with oriental enamel work, a coated stock of gleaming enamel finish bore the flawless reproductions. If embossing was represented, the reproductions were faultlessly embossed. A single issue might have 30 or more mag-

Christmas in My Bones

nificently reproduced art works, many of them masterworks, tipped in by hand and mounted on heavy matte pages tastefully bordered. Metallic stock and inks were used when desired, remaining untarnished and free of smudge.

We have other personal Christmas customs which give pleasure to our house. I mention these periodical imports, to which I could add domestic products – a complete file of the splendid *Golden Book* magazine which lived a decade prior to 1934, the last lovely issues of *Scribner's*, some old *Life*'s back to 1914 and several cherished books – all treasured, because in them I have a touchstone. I can find in them always, Christmas unchanged, happy, warm, jolly, prankish, bright, opulent and serene.

Christmas Beard

As the Christmas season approached one year I found myself sporting a beard, though there were some who would change the word "sporting" to something fairly scathing – there are always friends like that, but let it go.

Growing beards is a kind of hobby of mine. It's a marvelously easy hobby; it works while I sleep. I have never been much at raising vegetables or flowers but with beards I'm pretty good. I had hoped to use it in a couple of plays that fall, but had to cancel those plans. I still hoped to employ it in the interest of the theatre arts before the season passed, but as Christmas approached I was just wearing it.

I had had two or three beards in earlier years, but never one like this one. It was full. Virgin brush. Nary a razor or clipper had touched my face since the latter

Christmas in My Bones

part of August. This was no dapper set of chin whiskers, no mere goatee, but a growth which richly vegetated my jowls and would soon make a necktie unnecessary, even on Sunday.

This beard flourished like the green bay tree. And it was white. Or very nearly white. This was a condition which had come about since the last time I grew a beard. Though my facial foliage was never black, as my hair once was. When I had hair. It is a cotton-picking shame I can't do with the top of my head what I easily accomplish with the lower half.

I never had a beard at Christmas time before. That coupled with the fact that this one was full and white resulted in a whole new area of experience for me. Very small children regularly took me for Santa Claus. I rather enjoyed it.

In Greensboro I popped into Jay's Fine Foods one day to say hello to "Jay" and Marty Jacobs and wish them happy holiday. Near the door stood a father holding a pretty little girl who rewarded me – or at least my beard – with a smile and said "Hello, Santa Claus."

I received any number of such beatific smiles that Christmas season and they alone made the beard worthwhile. At the supermarket where I buy groceries and have almost my entire social life, I was repeatedly accepted as old Father Christmas himself. The children there did not usually speak to me first, but I would catch them staring at me in wide-eyed wonder and I knew what they were thinking. The dialogue that followed went something like this:

"Have you been a good little girl (or boy) this year?"

Nod of the head. Or a somewhat uncertain affirmative statement.

"Do you want me to come to see you this Christmas?"

More emphatic nod of the head, often accompanied by more enthusiastic affirmative statement.

"Well, write me a letter telling me what you want and be sure to show it to your parents before you mail it."

At this there was usually quite a wide, delighted smile, a vigorous nod and verbal assurance that such would be done.

My friends Jimmy and Shirley Swann had two little girls named Lisa and Kim. Lisa was about four and knew me. Kim was about 18 months old and did not know me. I was at their house one night when Kim entered the room and saw me. Her blue eyes grew round and great. She gazed at me in stunned unbelief and then with a wave winningly timid and a voice meeker than anyone has heard her employ since she uttered her first peep she said, "Hey, Sanny Claus."

We then went through the have-you-been-good and do-you-want-me-to-come-to-see-you-Christmas routine and Kim keeping her small voice answered "uh... ...huh" to each question, hesitating between the syllables in a most engaging way. But when I asked what she wanted, Kim found a firmer voice and I have seldom heard words roll from a child's mouth in such a torrent.

Lisa, on the other hand, was smugly sophisticated. She knew a thing or two. "Aw, you're not Santa Claus," she proclaimed, "I know you." I said "Of

Christmas in My Bones

course I am. I have two names. What do you think I do for a living?" She was suddenly converted. As Kim was dainty, Lisa was a cute little butter-ball of a girl with a voice that was deep and three times as big as she was. "Well, Lord, have mercy!" she boomed, "Let me get my catalog!"

She promptly dug out a well-worn Sears, Roebuck catalog and with practiced hand flipped it open to the toy section. "I want everything on this page," she said, "and everything on this page and...."

"Wait," I interrupted, "just give me the page numbers." She did and I took them down. I wished Jimmy and Shirley luck as I was leaving.

I got quite into the spirit of the thing. I did not – and still do not, it is true – have the girth usually associated with the role, but children seem willing to overlook that under the persuasion of the beard. Besides I could pad. I seriously considered booking a few chimneys for Christmas Eve. I was going to have cards printed saying, "Have Pillow, Will Travel."

Home for Christmas

Home for Christmas. The words danced in my mind along that distant and protracted highway out of Florida, up through Georgia, South Carolina and most of North Carolina. I knew the same words and the thousand accompanying thoughts were going through Martha's mind, too, although, since she did most of the driving, she had less time to enjoy them than I did.

Home for Christmas. There are few words in the language which contain excitement as well, a sort of quiet, cozy excitement, the joy of the familiar, faces, places, customs, images, all of the things that make one's so-called workaday world anything but commonplace, if viewed with the proper affectionate attention and appreciation. And, of course, at Christmas time all of it, the earth and sky and all they hold, are touched with a particular radiance.

Christmas in My Bones

We had been in Boca Raton, Florida, for six weeks while I performed in the new Caldwell Theatre's production of the Kaufman-Hart comedy, *You Can't Take It With You*. While there we enjoyed almost unblemished weather, with sunny days, and nights that varied from soothingly balmy to pleasantly cool. The sun, which had run up a very good shining average for December, was bright and hot. The beaches were populated, and I was assured by the population that the water was fine. I was willing to accept this appraisal and not test its accuracy.

The truth is that I have never been particularly amphibious and I seem to grow less so with the passage of time. The ocean is a fascinating and powerfully impressive quantity of liquid. I like to look at it. It stirs a certain urge with the thought that it is the cradle of life, but I have no inclination to be rocked in the cradle of the deep.

I know – I started out writing about Christmas, but I had a difficult time accepting that the Christmas season was indeed upon us while we were in Florida.

Every now and then Martha would say, "It just doesn't seem like Christmas," to which I usually would add the original and thought-provoking observation, "It certainly does not." It is all a matter of environmental adjustment, I expect. We were accustomed to Christmas higher on the map and lower in degrees Fahrenheit. It seems odd, if not downright improper, to see a Christmas wreath consorting with tropical vegetation. It seems equally odd to behold a Christmas tree salesman in a sport shirt mopping his brow in June-like sunlight.

W.C. "Mutt" Burton

There was sometimes the curious sensation that Christmas had, through some error of navigation, sailed off its course and foundered on a foreign shore. That is both unfair and unreasonable. Florida is, for instance, filled with evergreen firs, the Norfolk pine (which is so symmetrical and deep green that it looks artificial), the Australian pine and many others. Certainly palm trees are not alien to the Christmas image. Millions of Christmas cards for scores of years have carried pictures of the Holy Land and illustrations of the Christmas story, the Magi en route to the manger, representations of Bethlehem and artists' conceptions of the manger scene, all replete with palm trees. So Christmas is just as much at home there as anywhere, if indeed not more so.

But for Martha and me, home lay farther north where family and old friends awaited our return. On Monday, December 22, I packed the car for our return home wearing Bermuda shorts and a T-shirt.

We did not, it is true, leave Boca Raton without some pangs and a sad sense of parting. The people of Boca were even more pleasantly warm than the weather. First there was the Caldwell Theatre family, the members of which had made our 40-performance engagement a happy experience from beginning to end. It was not easy to say goodbye to them.

Furthermore Florida itself appeared to be putting on a farewell spectacle for us. It began to rain shortly after dark as we drew nearer the northern border, and we entered Georgia in a cold drizzle, but that last afternoon, homeward bound on the Florida Turnpike was something to remember.

Christmas in My Bones

It is probable that Palm Beach County, night and day, has the most spellbinding arrangement of sky and clouds to be found anywhere. The light is lovely, what with all that ocean to reflect and re-reflect its brilliance.

On this afternoon the light seemed to have been freshly washed, it was so crystal clear. The sky was a pure cerulean blue except for the decorations of cloud formations which swept along both east and west horizons, in blazing gold and crimson and mauve on the one hand, and softly tinted strands on the other. Ahead of us, with the highway heading directly into it, there were castles of dusky blue with foaming, mountainous packs of snowy, shining ranges rolling into infinity. And believe it or not, there was even a rainbow in the sky.

Then the light began to take on subtle and wonderful colors as the rays came from under the changing cloud canopies, amber and pink and gold by turns. It was a wonderful show. Still, home was an even brighter, more beckoning vision – and that lay beyond the cloud banks.

True, there would be some cherished Christmas touches missing. The door would be wreathless, though hospitable. The candles and holly and red ribbon would not be up on Christmas Eve. And it would mean a harried, crowded, exhausting day if we managed even a token display of the Yuletide adornment we like for our house by the small hours of Christmas Eve.

Not to mention the Christmas tree. That has always been the indispensable ornament of the season at our house, its lights glowing, its baubles glittering and seeming to fill our whole house as it stood in its rightful corner by the fireplace, its green, bedecked limbs spreading their mystical aura through all rooms. Well, we might have to have a treeless Christmas, as dismal as such a prospect seemed.

Treeless or not, home is the place to spend Christmas. This sentiment is an ingredient which flavors many of Charles Dickens' tales of the Yuletide. It has also been painted into pictures, made into verse and noted in song. For all its use and abuse, however, it is a fine old plum pudding of an axiom, and it is spiked with the mellow brandy of truth.

Home for Christmas. It is a phrase which evokes a cozy, rosy-cheeked mood – wayfarers bouncing back to their native cots over the snow-covered coach road, beaming faces around the fireplace, steaming bowl on the hearth, mistletoe over the doorway, holly in the windows, the pungent oven and the goose hanging high.

Actually the Christmas chimney corner is seldom a scene so serene since too frequently there is little time for glowing contentment and much too often the bright and tender season is heralded by scenes which more closely resemble a festival in bedlam.

There is, in fact, usually, a desperate rush to do far too many things in far too little time. We are so busy getting ready for Christmas Day that it arrives and departs before we can really observe it. Bills and tension mount in a heady whirl which sweeps us along in excitement, only to put us down in frustration, just out of reach of the Christmas Spirit.

Christmas in My Bones

Still, be it ever so helter-skelter, there's no place like home. That's where I have spent most of my already considerable number of Christmases and, though sometimes slightly dazed, I have enjoyed them all.

Two Christmases I have spent in barracks. One of these was passed on the windy, gray plains of Oklahoma. I can't recall much about it. I do remember that I was not rushed or pressed in any way. I was not afflicted with fuss or bother or last-minute Yule chores undone. I had plenty of time and a fair amount of quiet and tranquility. It was as hollow as the ho-ho-ho of a department store Santa and as dreary as his beard.

A Christmas tree was set up in the barracks and brightly decked upon company orders. The mess sergeant had whipped up a batch of cookies in the shapes of stars and Santa Claus and such, and these were hung on the green branches as edible ornaments. We exchanged gifts and sang some carols and called out the old greetings but in spite of the heartiest efforts of the special services officer, the festivities failed to fizz. An important element was missing: home.

On the following Christmas I was about as far away from home as a fellow can get unless he lives there – in India. Somehow I remember that time more clearly and somewhat more pleasantly. December in Bengal is a delightful month. The Indian climate, which for most of the year exhibits a horrid disposition, is on its sublimest behavior from the middle of November until the middle of March, mild and fair. Daily the skies are unclouded azure and the sun is brilliant but gentle.

W.C. "Mutt" Burton

This particular Christmas Day of 1944, was a jewel of a day. But it did not seem real. It seemed canned and imported, like the turkey we had for Christmas dinner. It was like moving, awake and aware, through an exotic dream of Christmas Day.

There was a big evergreen in the mess hall, trimmed with genuine tinsel and gay globules of glass – but it was the most foreign-looking piece of shrubbery I ever saw in my life.

I kept thinking of the Rudyard Kipling poem, "Christmas in India." Not the whole poem and not in its sense of irony and tinge of bitterness. All I could remember was the first line: "Dim dawn behind the tamarisks – the sky is saffron yellow." It was a strangely detached piece of word music and it seemed a theme which set the mood of the whole day for me.

On the afternoon of Christmas Day some of us, for reasons which do not return to me at the moment, procured a jeep and toured the tortured little alleys of Calcutta. The domes and odd spires of buildings, the palm trees standing still against the afternoon sky, made pictures which suggested the colored prints on the walls of Sunday School rooms back home.

I thought this was, perhaps, more nearly the native scenery of Christmas than any setting in which I had ever celebrated the season.

This, too, was a tranquil Christmas, this Christmas in India. The day held a spacious hush as its colors changed slowly and delicately from morning until night. But it never achieved the real glow of a Christmas Day.

I prefer as a regular thing, however, the frosty

Christmas in My Bones

brightness and the cozy cheer of a winter Christmas and a home Christmas. I'll light my candles in my own windows and my tree in its familiar corner and have what serenity I can manage under my own roof.

Weary, but relieved and glad, Martha and I came into the familiar streets of Reidsville, our old and ailing AMC Matador loaded with such a cargo as no Gypsy ever envisioned. Quite apart from the luggage of necessity, clothing for hot, warm and cool days, the customary personal and medical accoutrements, there were Christmas gifts which had to be transported home since all shopping had to be done in Florida.

There was a fairly large plastic coolbox filled with avocados and papayas from the trees of our friends the Pat Pattersons in West Palm Beach. There was a huge plastic bag filled with cutting from all manner of Florida flora, which Martha hoped to root for house growth. And there were, so help me, two potted plants and an armful of eucalyptus obtained from a garden on St. Simons Island, Georgia, for aromatic dried arrangements, the last-named items enveloping my feet most of the way home.

But at last, at shortly after 9 p.m. on December 23, we pulled up in front of Payment Downs, as we appropriately dubbed our modest abode when we bought it, and halted the freight of voyaging at our home port, our fractional estate. We were home for Christmas.

To our pleasant surprise, our advent stars were shining in the windows. The carriage light wore a bright red bow, and the front door was adorned with a fresh red-bowed wreath. And there, when we unlocked and entered, in its rightful corner, stood our

W.C. "Mutt" Burton

fresh-from-the-mountain-tops Christmas tree, fully dressed in its traditional jewelry as usual and promptly put to shedding the cheerful colors of its many electric bulbs. There were candles and greenery and adornments about. And soon, so were our children and grandchildren, though they had obviously spent a great deal of time there before our arrival.

Home for Christmas. Three wonderful words with wondrous meaning. No other three can come up to them – except perhaps, I love you. And, come to think of it, they really mean the same thing.

Christmas Morning

The sternest sort of resolution to the contrary notwithstanding, I arrived one particular Christmas Eve in exactly the same condition which has obtained at this time every year since I can remember, physically and financially depleted (not a very long process of depletion in either case), way behind in my customary race with time, breathless, desperate and frantic in my effort to put everything in apple-pie order for the Yuletide.

I failed, of course.

I was going to have all my packages wrapped three days before Christmas. That I resolved to do, my chin set firmly and a steely glint of determination in my eyes. As it turned out I finished my shopping after six p.m. Christmas Eve and did not even start wrapping packages until after 1 a.m. Christmas Day.

W.C. "Mutt" Burton

A few of the gifts I bought were beautifully gift-wrapped in the shops and stores where purchased, but so many of the things I get for gifts are obtained in marts where gift-wrapping is considered a fantastic luxury. Anyway, I started out being reasonably careful, putting little touches here and there, bows, fancy foils, cards to harmonize with the wrappings, things like that. As the hour grew later and later, my approach to the concept of the artistically concealed Christmas gift became increasingly cavalier. By four a.m. I was in a furious hassle with plain white tissue and cellophane tape, and the packages looked as if they had been wrapped by a wheat binder.

I tumbled into bed at six a.m. and I was tumbled out again for the family Christmas tree at 9:30. That was three hours more sleep than I got when our daughters were younger, but in those days I, too, was younger.

With a mighty summoning of practically superhuman will power I shook off the heavy dregs of sleep and gazed out with bilious, glazed and blood-shot eyes upon a clear, chill Christmas morning. I did not dare look into a mirror, but I had the feeling that my eyes looked like two soft-boiled eggs with a tablespoon of port wine poured over each.

Moving with the dazed, stiff, unheeding mobility pattern of a zombie, I pulled a pair of pants on over my pajamas, slipped into, or more correctly, staggered into the hallway and pondered with grave misgivings my ability to navigate the staircase.

By the time I reached the living room, circulation was being restored to my body, at least that portion of

Christmas in My Bones

it below the neck, though I still moved awkwardly and more out of a long-established memory of what I had to do than out of the dictates of my conscious mind. At that hour my conscious mind could not have dictated the opening stanza of "Baby Bye, sees a fly."

Gradually, however, I got the fire laid and lighted. I plugged in the Christmas tree lights and put matches to the numerous candles with which Martha had prepared the room for the festive season. When the room was a cheerful blaze and glow, with the flames in the fireplace licking up hungrily around the logs, I began to feel some kindred spark of life within me, though it fell on the sodden kindling of my depleted tissues where it could do no more than smolder.

Martha and our daughters, Martha Jane and Anna B., who were waiting in the kitchen, and restoring their souls with coffee, came into the living room when I had completed my numbly accomplished ceremonials of Christmas morning. By tradition, Martha Jane takes the gifts from under the tree and passes them out to us. I sank leadenly into my chair by the fireplace, feeling the warmth of firelight on my face and a conviction in my innermost being that I might remain anchored in that chair, night and day, for at least a week.

It was a fine Christmas morning, despite my enervated condition. It was a fine moment in the finest of all days of the year. I opened my own Christmas gifts with surprise and delight and watched with equal delight as Martha and our girls opened their presents. So haphazardly coordinated were my mental functions that I found I was surprised at some of the gifts I had bought for them.

W.C. "Mutt" Burton

Among the gifts which I received with pleasure were three pipes, two of them among the finest I have ever owned, a superbly gadgety tool from a friend who knows my special fondness for superbly gadgety tools and several other splendid things, including a few toys. Even at my advanced age I still enjoy playing and I pity the fellow who does not.

Martha always had a kind of genius for selecting and, sometimes, designing and making gifts for me that were positively just the ticket, and Martha Jane and Anna B. show the same sort of understanding. From them I got a tricky game of skill, a top – a beautiful walnut top made by mountain craftsmen of North Carolina; a handsome lap robe (heaters or no, I like to tuck my shanks in if I am riding in the back seat of a car in winter); a hand vacuum that is perfect for cleaning the dust out of my darkroom, off of photographic equipment and off book shelves; a neat pen knife that has an unbelievably dainty, but precise and useful pair of scissors in one blade cradle and other items without which my life would, obviously, be incomplete.

Best of all was the shared gift of being together, under our own roof and within our own walls, of having one another and a home. So it mattered little as I wrote about it on the far fag end of Christmas Day that I was tired, weary, fatigued, exhausted, done in, worn out, spent, winded, pooped, beat, bushed and hors de combat.

But next year....

A Christmas Story

𝕴 came upon this story some 60 years ago in the writings of Sir Philip Gibbs, a British journalist and novelist who was popular in the 1920s, but who is now no longer read except, possibly, by a loyal and scattered few. Fact or fable, the story is, to me, unfailingly moving. I have used it in speeches, told it to friends and used at least a part of it in writings several times. It has been retold by others. It does not matter. It needs telling and retelling. Over and over again.

If memory serves, the strange and beautiful moment was witnessed by Sir Philip himself, with unbelieving and perhaps misted eyes. It is a Christmas story, in some ways the most dramatic, the most miraculous, the most mysterious I have ever heard, except that of the Nativity itself. From another view, however, its happenings were perfectly understandable, especially if you are among those hopefuls who hold that man, though a grievously flawed creature, is susceptible of salvage. From any view it seems to me marvelous and moving.

I shall have to set the story down from memory; I would not know where to find it now. This presents no problem, however, since the story, in its essentials, has remained with me since I first read it many years ago. It shows, better than any story I can think of, the heartless stupidity, the incredible folly of man's practice of war. And it shows that Christmas is, above all, a season of the heart.

The time was Christmas Eve 1917, and the birth of the Prince of Peace was brutally observed. The First World War was tearing the world apart. The place was a battlefield in Europe, a fringe of the war where the front lines were so close that no-man's land between the German and Allied trenches was hardly wider than a fair-sized lawn.

It was a clear night. The stars were out, twinkling wistfully above the din of carnage, but hardly visible through the drifting smoke of battle. If the Star of the East had appeared that night, shining even more brilliantly than it had shone over Bethlehem, it might easily have gone unnoticed by the men below, burrowed into the ground like rodents, firing their rifles and mortars at strangers whom they had nothing against.

Not only would the Star have been obscured by smoke, it would have suffered the blinding competition of shell bursts, artillery fire aimed from some remote distance, impersonally designed to inflict hap-

Christmas in My Bones

hazard death and destruction, hopefully on the "enemy."

As the hour drew near midnight, the firing began to wither. The crackle of rifles came halfheartedly and at increasingly longer intervals from both sides. A last artillery shell burst with a flash and a boom that swelled into an enveloping silence. And suddenly all firing ceased.

There had been no earthly order to cease fire. Perhaps these armed, uniformed and weary men had been moved by a concerted impulse, a consciousness of the day and its meaning. Perhaps it had come to them that their's was strange behavior for humanity, and a surpassingly inappropriate way to celebrate the birthday of the Child of Peace.

For a few moments the men in the trenches remained motionless, as if stunned. The smoke sifted away into the crisp, clear December night and the men could see the stars. Some soldiers thought one star, there toward the east, shone brighter than the others.

Only a short stretch of scarred land lay between the front line trenches of the Germans and those of the allies, English, Americans and a scattering of French. A doughboy broke out a battered harmonica and began to play, softly at first, that most beloved of carols, "Silent Night, Holy Night...All is calm, all is bright," and suddenly a German youth climbed out of the slit earth, stood on the edge of his trench, his form outlined against the star-spattered horizon, and sang the song in a fine, clear tenor, "Stille Nacht, Heilige Nacht..." the music floated toward the stars.

After a moment a young Englishman responded

with "It Came Upon a Midnight Clear," which encouraged a sergeant from Montgomery, Alabama, to try out his soft baritone on "O, Little Town of Bethlehem."

The song finished, an English soldier, an irrepressible cockney, ventured a tentative, "Merry Christmas, Fritz," and the greeting came back in surprisingly good English, "Merry Christmas." As if this had been a prearranged signal, the men, German, English, American, French, piled out of the trenches and began to walk, without fear, toward one another.

They came alone and by twos – and then by half-dozens and dozens, calling out greetings – "Merry Christmas" in the different languages the men brought from their homelands. They shook hands, clapped one another on the shoulder and babbled in their separate tongues with a common understanding, relief and joy. They filled that little plot of empty doom called no-man's land with the spirit of all men of good will. They laughed like children. Some of them shouted and danced, and a few of them wept.

And they exchanged Christmas gifts, employing for this festivity all they could offer, the pocket trinkets and miscellany that men carry about with them, pen knives, fountain pens, cigarettes, bits of chocolate – and they thanked one another in merry gratitude and separate tongues and accents for these wonderful gifts, for they were treasures beyond price.

This joyous sanity might have continued far into the night but somehow the unbelievable report filtered back to field headquarters and a stern command was sent up – this amiable frivolity was most unwarlike and possibly an outrage. It must stop at once. The men

must return to their trenches and resume mortal combat immediately.

This order – to put the spirit of Christmas on hold and take up arms again – did it come from "our side" or "their side?" It doesn't matter. The soldiers obeyed reluctantly, half-heartedly, bidding each other their rueful good nights. They went back to their memories of home with the clear conviction that they had experienced a night they would never forget. Firing began again, eventually, to appease the military machine. But the men knew they were no longer shooting at strangers.

So, it is shown that the first casualties of war are reason and decency. But it is also a heartening reminder that man's spirit can rise above the most dismal conditions.

It was only a brief miracle, but no less wonderful. Out of the murder, madness and havoc, for a time, a short but forever unforgettable time to those men, there had come peace and joy and good will. Because it was Christmas. Christmas on a blasted, bloody field.

If the spirit of that mysterious night had been allowed to spread unabated it would have put the war out of business. It might even have achieved the end proclaimed in our popular war motto. It might have made "the world safe for democracy."

The Days of Christmas

The morning comes, rosy,
Not early, but bright,
In lacy cap and petticoat,
With hard, cold breath,
Like an old lady with a sharp nose,
But ruddy cheeks and merry eyes.
The morning crackles underfoot
And its grass breaks like glass.
The fresh day shines in the sun,
And the crusty earth blinks,
While wooded places stir reluctantly,
Pull their lingering darkness close
And snuggle under dry layers of leaves,
To snatch a few more winks of sleep
Than the clearing gets.

W.C. "Mutt" Burton

Houses shut tight against the night
Crack open in the morning sun
And crystal light,
And let the people out
To move about,
To start the new day's work.
Faces grow rosier than the east.
Breath rolls out in smoky vapors
And the smell of hot, gulped coffee –
As incense to the altar of the East.

Down the block an automobile,
Icy pile on polished steel,
Coughs against the winter's grip,
Rips the silence among the houses
Along the street.
It roars to limber up its sluggish pistons
To warm its oily blood
And go growling and
Snarling away down town,
Spitting fumes from the deepest pits
Of Texas, Oklahoma and Pennsylvania,
And belching smoke, a dyspeptic dragon,
Eager to reach the field of conflict
And fight for a parking space.

It is a winter day being born,
In some ways like any winter day
Opening up for business,
Setting up shop,
Doing its regular job.

Christmas in My Bones

But it is not just any winter day
Or just any old time
In the winter season.
One knows.
One knows.
One can tell –
Or, anyway, any child can tell,
No matter how young or old.

There is in this air a special lightness
And in this light a special brightness,
And in the clearness laughter newly tuned.
There is a quiet singing in this day.

High noon with high heart
Comes to split the day apart
And point the shadows north.
Time, suspended, hangs in even lustre,
Serene and clean against the trees and walls,
And, moving westward with the sun,
Brings afternoon and dusk – and day is done.
It moves too fast? You'd have it stay?
It goes to start another day.

Watch the day,
Watch the night.
Don't let them go unseen.
Look at the light,
Walk with it across a field
Or see it falling through a window,
Changing, forming visions, colors,

W.C. "Mutt" Burton

Inside and out, a magic potion
Spilling from the sky.
See the evening exhibition
Unparalleled, beyond compare.
Behold great boulders of clouds
Turn gold, then silver, then vanish,
While the moon and stars hang gleaming
In the Magician's purple scarf –
And presto! Night!
Night, steely blue and shivered
With piercing stars and jewel moon.

Surely you can tell from this,
The way the day in radiance goes,
The way the very darkness glows.
Why is this wonderment of earth and sky?
These are the days of Christmas – that is why.
They are filled with the feel
And sights and sounds of Christmas
With ancient mysteries and words
And promises from ages past
And echoes from forgotten years.

These days have a lilt, a chime
Of caroling from time to time,
From dawn's white crest, down night's far slope,
They shine for Noel – birth – new hope!

Letter to Santa

𝕴 don't know whether Santa Claus has been a regular reader (or even an infrequent one) of the newspaper column I have written for more than half a century, but in the event he was, one Christmas I decided to do my two young daughters the fatherly favor of passing on to him, in that space, a few advance suggestions on what they wanted for Christmas. Though that was nearly forty years ago, and my daughters – and now even my grandchildren – have long since opted for a more direct means of informing Santa of their desires, I have kept that letter. I suspect that despite the passing years similar lists are formed every year by children captured by the Christmas rapture – and always will be.

Martha Jane, age 8, wants a bicycle, Saint

Nicholas. She wants a few other things, including an electric train, but the heavily-underlined item on her list is a bike. She has mentioned this several hundred times in the past few weeks and she has taken to requesting it in her prayers, especially the ones she utters under the supervision of her mother or me. I consider that a pretty broad hint.

Now I'll tell you, Nick (column writers always call celebrities by their first names, a rule of the trade), I'm not entirely free of qualms about that bike. Too many people drive too many automobiles too fast. However, she vows, with such intensity that she closes her eyes and compresses her lips, that she will be very, very careful always, so I am not going to put my foot down against it.

I think I should tell you, too, that she has decided to be big about it. She told me just the other evening, "Now listen, daddy, I'm going to tell you what I've decided and I hope it will make you happy, because it took courage to do it. I mean it took courage." She said the word "courage" with a great deal of vigor, contorting her face, to show me just how much courage it took.

"I want a bicycle," Martha Jane continued, "that's what I really want – and if Santa Claus brings me one I'll be happy. I reckon I'll be about the happiest person you ever saw. But...(here she paused, summoning the aforementioned courage) if Santa Claus doesn't bring me a bicycle (she very nearly shuddered here), why that's going to be all right. I'm going to take what he brings me, whatever it is, and I'm going to treasure it." She said the word "treasure" with much intensity,

Christmas in My Bones

too. No use making a noble speech unless you give it the works.

Still feeling the pleasant intoxication of her virtuous philosophy, she added "I've made up a saying about this: What is going to be is going to be." I'm not wholly sure of the originality of her "saying," but I think it shows a very decent attitude, Nick, pretty fine for a girl who was eight years old last April. I gave her a good proud hug.

Of course, Martha Jane is old enough to know that your services are not absolutely free. She is aware that you cannot operate a toy shop, even at the North Pole, where building and rental costs are much lower than they are here, without some overhead. She knows the reindeer have to be fed, the harness and sleigh kept in good repair and your tailor doesn't turn out those snappy red suits for nothing.

Because of this and several attendant circumstances which I am sure you appreciate, I have made no final commitment on the bicycle, either for you or me. I just thought I'd brief you on the situation to see what you could do about it. You know, just in case you have a bike that you can spare, one that would fit a fairly long-legged eight-year-old girl who is willing to be reasonable about the whole thing.

Nick, I don't know whether you remember about our chimney. It is broken up into three separate flues and, in addition to that, it is rigged with a TV antenna and an FM antenna.

This situation is rather common these days, I suppose, but if you do bring a bike it might be especially awkward. You'd better, if you bring one, just roll it in the basement door. I'm pretty sure Martha Jane would find it. Not that she's expecting it, you understand. Just in case.

While I am about it, Nick, old pal, old buddy, I'd like to remind you that I have done business with you for several years now. I've always given my Christmas business to you and I'd appreciate any little courtesy you could extend to me in the way of discounts, service fees, etc. The coffee and cookies, by the way, will be on the mantel as usual, and if you'd like a little more substantial snack just let me know.

So far I haven't said anything about what Anna B, age 4, wants, but there's no great problem there. She did say something to me about wanting a record player, and dolls are a mighty-good staple with her, but she has also expressed a desire to have you bring her maybe a thousand other things. When I ask her what she wants for Christmas her eyes light up and it is some time before she stops talking. I'd say the regular blue-plate special for four-year-old girls would do the trick, Nick. You name it, she wants it.

As a general report on the conduct of both Martha Jane and Anna B., I can say that they have been very good girls most of the time. Sometimes their behavior is angelic, but, of course, at an average level it would be fairer to say that they behave well except when they are disturbed by some unusual circumstance like not getting their own way.

Speaking for our entire family, we shall expect your visit not later than the evening of December 24 or the early morning of December 25 and, as Martha Jane put it, we will "treasure" whatever you bring.

Christmas in My Bones

I convey to you our affectionate regards, especially those of Martha Jane and Anna B., who do their Christmas wishing early.

Christmas Fireworks

Rummaging about under the eaves of our house not long ago I came upon a box which bore a faded Railway Express Agency label on one side and two other labels on the top. Some things that I wanted to save had been stored away in this corrugated-cardboard box. I hadn't seen it in years.

It is strange what small fragments will trigger memory, a whiff of perfume, a strain of music, a face glimpsed in a crowd, an old cardboard shipping case with faded labels. The box is 11 inches wide, 17 inches long and 10 inches deep. It is about 45 years old. There are no dates on it, but I can place it pretty well, give or take a year or two, by the labels. It is the labels on top which prompt the memory most particularly.

Seeing them the other day, I could feel for a moment the intense and joyous excitement they had

Christmas in My Bones

stirred in my youthful bosom those many years ago. The box came just before Christmas. It would be difficult for me to convey the fullness of delight and excitement with which I welcomed the express man who brought it.

Even the address label moved me to a deep and greedy happiness. The address said "William C. Burton, 328 Piedmont Street, Reidsville, N.C." It thrilled me to read it because it meant the contents of that box were mine, all mine to set fire to. The printed matter on the label (it was a red and white label with blue decoration) immediately disclosed its contents. It is just possible, however, that you would have had to be a boy living in a small town in the South at Christmas time in the early 1920s to get even a glimmer of light on why the arrival of this box made me dance and whoop like an Indian.

Along the top margin of the label ran the words: "CELEBRATION GOODS – RUSH." It was a dark red label filled with black-printed warnings which made fascinating reading on that Christmas long past. It said "FIREWORKS – HANDLE CAREFULLY – KEEP FIRE AWAY – DO NOT DROP NOR THROW" (the label was concerned with being emphatic rather than grammatical). Under that the sending firm's name appeared. It was Spencer Fireworks Co. Spencer Fireworks Co., firm of revered recollection. What terrible thunder and delectable dangers you brought the boys of my generation.

There was in the time of my boyhood a custom which may strike those foreign to our neck of the woods as strange, but it was cherished in the Southeast

— the shooting of Christmas firecrackers. I believe we thought of it, though not consciously, as a "joyful noise unto the Lord," since it certainly was a joyful noise unto us — particularly those of us who were young and male. I am not quite sure what young girls in general thought about firecrackers except that I recall a tendency on their part to stop up their ears against the detonation of the loud items which were called "salutes" or "bombs." Naturally, the inevitable squeals and even screams of girls when boys tossed lighted "squibs" at their feet were taken for granted as feminine weaknesses.

I am bound to admit that such aggressive actions with firecrackers must be considered reprehensible but it seemed a moderately pleasing diversion at the time. Was there a tinge of delight in those cries of fright? I don't know. An unconscious vestige of atavism, perhaps, on both sides. Surely it was not in keeping with the attributed "good will" of those holidays. (But didn't the familiar text say "good will toward men"? Didn't say a thing about girls.)

I must explain some details to the uninitiated in North Carolina, where for many years now the sale of fireworks has been forbidden by law and the shooting thereof suppressed. Squibs (which were called "Mandarin Crackers" on the label but not by us) were small, about the size of a sucker stick, and an inch or slightly more in length. They had fast paper fuses which were woven together by a common fuse and were meant to be shot off all at once. In that way they made a fine, rapid, machine-gun sort of popping which was very satisfactory, but to us it was unthinkably extrav-

Christmas in My Bones

agant. They were shot that way to celebrate the Chinese New Year (by the Chinese but not by us.)

No, sir. We carefully unraveled them and shot them one by one, even though a string of 100 cost only 15 cents in the old days. Some boys, against parental orders held squibs by the tip end and let them go off, attesting to their bravery with tingling fingers. Salutes were available in two, three and five-inch sizes and were half an inch or more in diameter. The five-inchers were choice, but more costly. The real prizes were the bombs, chiefly the "Cherry Bomb," which was coated with some silvery metallic substance and was equally mighty.

You could send off a money order for $3 to Spencer Fireworks Company and receive by railway express a wooden box bigger than a shoe box, crammed full of glitter bombs.

I do not remember the contents of the box in detail but I can say with assurance that it was filled chiefly with a certain small, but powerful, noisemaker much in favor with me and with my companions of like age and disposition in those days. It was a silver salute, a cylinder about an inch long and half-an-inch in diameter with a good long fabric fuse. It was covered with a silvery metallic coating and contained some substance variously alleged by its devotees to be TNT, nitroglycerin, dynamite or a "secret formula."

There were "Torpedoes," which were twists of paper containing gravel and a fairly large paper "cap," which were pleasant when hurled against the sidewalk. "Devils-On-the-Walk" (which we called "spit devils") were the size of checkers and made of a hard compound. They spat with a rattling chain of minor explosions when scratched along a stone wall or the cement sidewalk. Ground under foot against the sidewalk (which gave them their catalogue label), they made a greater cracking, but your shoe soles had better not be thin or it would tremble your toes.

The display of night pieces, Vesuvius Fountains, pinwheels and the like were outside our modest budgets, though we sometimes bought a few smaller Roman Candles and skyrockets. So, our Christmas pyrotechnics were mostly audible. For the visual variety (with plenty of noise, too, including block-shattering "dago bombs") we in our neighborhood enjoyed the really impressive spectacle put on each Christmas Eve by Mr. Charlie Penn, who was a vice-president of the American Tobacco Co. and believed in doing things right. The night sky above his mansion, which centered our block, was, on each Christmas Eve, a dazzling canopy of fiery jewelry.

The truth be told, however, in our innermost hearts we boys preferred the big bang and power of the salutes and bombs, which would send a tin can sky-high or tear it open and bend it inside out, the sound bouncing back from every house in the neighborhood. Our neighborhood was literally littered with contorted tin cans during the Christmas holidays. Maybe we preferred the more audible variety of fireworks because it shattered the anticlimax that followed the opening of the presents, when there was nothing new left in Christmas for a boy, but I think it satisfied a deeper natural urge in celebration, which was neither sacrilegious nor rowdy in our view.

Christmas in My Bones

In my boyhood, nightfall on Christmas Eve was greeted thunderously. Somewhere in the distance a man, moved by the Christmas spirit, and perhaps other spirits, would fire a shotgun into the air or (some said) let go with a stick of dynamite. Midnight reverberated with Yuletide artillery.

And Christmas Day was even noisier. Christmas Day, especially in the morning, sounded like two artillery outfits joined in combat. Heavy explosions rocked our block and echoing bursts could be heard in the next block and the next and the next and so on until the volleying died away in the rumbling distance.

I am glad that Christmas Eve in our town no longer reverberates with explosions near and far from sunset until the dawn of Christmas Day

I like the quiet Christmas time better, I'll admit. I am sure that the unhampered use of fireworks caused some injuries. It is only truth, however, to aver that I cannot recall ever witnessing such an injury or even knowing personally of such a happening. Apart from a few swollen fingers on the hands of foolhardy boys who wanted to show their daring by lighting two-inch salutes while holding them, I recall no fireworks injuries at all.

I love quiet and peace. I am solidly for safety and caution. I would regret the return of wholesale holiday cannonading. Still, I guiltily cherish a memory of Christmas with joyous noise.

Christmas Greenery

If you are, as you should be, a faithful observer of the Twelve Days of Christmas, you keep a good deal of greenery in your house – the traditional conifer with its gaudy trimmings, sprigs, sprays and swags of boxwood, pine, fir and hemlock, most likely magnolia if you live in the South, perhaps running cedar, doubtless a bit of mistletoe and, of course, holly.

It may interest you to know that, besides embellishing your domicile, some of these evergreens have properties you wouldn't believe. Or maybe you would. The ancients did.

Mistletoe and holly are especially versatile. They provide all manner of medications, panaceas, potions and the like. They ward off evil spirits and provide a sanctuary in the home for sylvan spirits – who haven't much place else to go in the winter. The Druids

Christmas in My Bones

wouldn't have been caught without a little mistletoe in the medicine cabinet.

Evil has also been done with mistletoe. You may recall that Balder, the good and beautiful son of the great Norse god, Odin, was slain with an apparently harmless sprig of mistletoe. In case you need a refresher on this case of deicide, Balder had dreams that seemed to forebode his death. The gods held council and exacted promises from practically everything animal, vegetable and mineral that they would not harm Balder. After that, for sport, the gods would get Balder to hold still while they hacked at him threw and shot things at him. It was a lot of fun and Balder enjoyed it, too, because nothing would hurt him.

Then Loki, the mischievous god, found out that the mistletoe plant had not been asked to take the be-kind-to-Balder oath because the gods thought it was too young to swear.

Naturally Loki got a sprig of mistletoe, persuaded someone to shoot it at Balder and zap!

For exterminating vampires, mistletoe and holly are indispensable. If you are expecting Count Dracula as a house guest you might want a little of both on hand.

There are about two dozen species of mistletoe. It abounds on oak trees in the United States, but also grows on other plants, including the Creosote bush. In England and France it grows chiefly on apple trees and is found very rarely on oaks. Druids, however, preferred oak-grown mistletoe to all others.

Pliny wrote of the veneration which the people of Gaul felt for mistletoe, especially the Druids, "for so they call their wizards." It was regarded as a universal healer, especially effective in the cure of epilepsy, ulcers and children's diseases. The ancient Italians, Japanese and Swedes all agreed that mistletoe was better than vitamins. Furthermore if a woman carried around a sprig of mistletoe on her person she was enabled to bear children.

The Walos of Senegambia carried mistletoe leaves on their persons when they went to war, as talismans to ward off wounds. Mistletoe doesn't rate such admiration in modern medical practice, but the AMA may change its mind about that later. As internal medicine, a tea was brewed, usually from the leaves. Joseph E. Meyer, in his book *The Herbalist*, notes mistletoe's reputation for stimulating properties of a high order, but warns against a dosage stronger than one teaspoonful to a pint of boiling water.

The best thing about mistletoe, however, is, in my opinion, that you can kiss pretty girls under it.

Holly is just about as magical a plant as mistletoe, if not more so. It, too, was long ago regarded as an aid to fertility and as such was given to newlyweds. Holly is also a symbol of eternal life; its name derived from the fact that it was once regarded as holy. Holly, like mistletoe, bestows kissing privileges. In the old days, during the Roman celebration of Saturnalia, a young man who caught a girl under a holly wreath could go as far as he liked with her.

In the Middle Ages, holly tea was employed as a cure for gout, gallstones, skin trouble and broken bones. It may surprise you to know that holly tea was given to the allied troops as a stimulant during World

Christmas in My Bones

War I and that it is now sold commercially in this country. No one should grab a handful of Christmas wreath and start brewing his own holly tea; it is potent and can be dangerous if the person doing the brewing doesn't know what he's doing.

American Indians made their tomahawk handles of holly wood and pioneer carpenters in America used it as a substitute for iron for making hinges and bolts. George Washington had a set of false teeth made of the ivory-like white wood of the holly.

In a fine article on holly in the December 1966 issue of *True* magazine, Daniel P. Mannix observes that "North Carolina is a great state for holly...." At the Holly Museum in Milleville, New Jersey, which calls itself The Holly City and is the capital of the holly growing industry in the U.S., there is a Nativity scene hand carved of holly wood from North Carolina. A holly tree in eastern North Carolina, now fallen, once was known as the grandfather of all hollies. It stood 72 feet in height and was 11 feet in circumference.

Holly hucksters, seeking Christmas profits, almost rendered holly extinct in the U.S., but the Holly Society of America and the Ashumet Holly Reservation at East Falmouth on Cape Cod, Massachusetts, properly conducted commercial orchards, and some dedicated amateur holly fanciers saved the day.

Oregon has the biggest orchards. A holly grower can get 2,000 pounds of holly per acre when his trees are fifteen years old and sell it for a handsome profit.

Holly is dioecious, that is it has male and female trees. Honey bees serve as the messengers of Cupid and one male tree can fertilize about 15 female trees, the only berry bearers. The *Encyclopaedia Britannica* says there are 180 species of holly. Mannix says there are 400.

In any case, Darwin once wrote of the holly, "During several years I have examined many plants, but have never found one that was really hermaphrodite." Well, that's a relief.

The Heart of Christmas

Plans partly or completely made,
Promptly started or delayed,
Lists of names and gifts begun,
Checked and rechecked one by one,
Looking up of old addresses,
Secrets formed against all guesses,
Digging out the decorations,
Adding new elaborations,
Buying wrappings, ribbons, tapers,
Santa's picture in the papers,
Snowy scenes in magazines,
Fireside sets on TV screens,
Picking out the Christmas cards,
Buying tinsel by the yards,
Making wreaths of yew and holly
And mistletoe (and feeling jolly,)
Writing 'til your hand has cramps,

W.C. "Mutt" Burton

Licking envelopes and stamps,
Mailing out the sentiments
That once cost three, now 29, cents –
> *These are the start of Christmas.*

Forays on the grocery store,
Nuts and sugar plums galore,
Fruits and cookies, candy, cake
To tempt the taste and tummy ache,
Hams and turkeys – goodbye diet –
Bake it, roast it, broil it, fry it,
Oysters, roast and stew and pan some
(Higher than a pirate's ransom,)
And, if you wish, a jug of wine
To taste when time has come to dine –
> *That's a la carte at Christmas.*

Roaming stores, mile after mile,
Up one row and down one aisle
Searching for the perfect gift,
Abandon caution, forfeit thrift.
Seize it, charge it, for today
The reckoning seems far away.
What joy it is going overboard
And buying what you can't afford.
(When Christmas Day is at its peak
Bills still won't come for another week.)
Now you've got your shopping done
For everybody – oops! – save one,
So, tired but game, you don your coat
And wrapping muffler 'round your throat –
> *Go back to the mart at Christmas.*

Christmas in My Bones

It's time to decorate the tree
And though you're weary as can be,
You fit the fir into its stand
And drape it then with strand on strand
Of shining tinsel, loops of light,
And hang each limb with bauble bright,
Wrap the gifts, each size and shape,
With wrappings gay and sticky tape
(Helping each holder of DuPont stock
To fatten up his Christmas sock).
Put the gifts, each shape and size,
Under the tree for the big surprise.
Clean the house and set it straight,
It's Christmas Eve and growing late.
You're dead for sleep and nearly numb,
Sore of foot and sore of thumb.
And as you sink into a chair
You feel a tinge of slight despair
And start a little to repent
The sums of money you have spent –
         This, too, is part of Christmas.

Then Christmas Day dawns as of old
And all it touches turns to gold.
The children shout with pure joy
Uncovering some wished-for toy,
And faces glow and hands touch hands
And heartstrings play like German bands,
And loved ones who are far away
Come sit in your heart this day.
Mem'ries crowd into your mind

W.C. "Mutt" Burton

Of Christmas Days you've left behind,
Dear friends recalled with warm affection
And carols sing through recollection.
Think of the Babe born in a manger
And do some kindness for a stranger.
When all seems hopeless, never cease
To hope for good will and for peace –
          For of such is the heart of Christmas.

Christmas Shopping

A day has a way of slipping away from me. I've had many a day just vanish right out from under me, leaving me to wonder what the Sam Hill exactly had happened to it.

It isn't that I don't try to fill the day with shining hours of accomplishment. I do try – every now and then. And I often resolve to try more often.

It is not particularly unusual for me to arise full of firm resolve and, what's more, filled with confidence that on this very day at whose threshold I stand I can and will do all of the things I have planned to do that day. And maybe one or two extra things in the bargain.

It is a fine feeling with which to begin the day. I feel ambitious, creative, efficient. In my mind's eye I catch a sort of exhilarating preview of the day in which I see myself clipping through each and every hour,

Christmas in My Bones

attending to this, seeing about that, getting several chores done and well done and with such dispatch.

It is a shame that the day never looks the same from its other end. It is like looking through the two ends of a telescope. At its beginning you look at the day through the small or proper end of the telescope. And the day looks big and bright and shining with promise.

In the evening you look back at the day through the big end of the telescope and it looks small – so small and vanishing (which it is). And the things you have accomplished are so small that you can hardly see them at all. Remembering the way it looked that morning you'd never think it was the same day.

Let us take for example Christmas shopping. It is more than appropriate; it is pressing. I can – and do – hustle up an extra charge of energy and determination to get this done.

It is about the Christmas season, as a matter of fact, that I want to do and have to do and need to do so many things that they begin to pile up on me the way ice blocks pile up on the banks of a river in the flood of a spring thaw. I begin to make notes for myself before going to bed at night.

These are very stern notes and they grow sterner, more imperative each day. Many of these lists are headed "MUST" or "Must Do Today!!!"

Under such no-nonsense headings I list all manner of chores: stories I have been putting off writing, letters I have been putting off writing, checks I have been putting off writing, errands to run, things I must buy because they are things which our household cannot possibly function a single day without and we haven't any – and haven't had for the past two months.

You know what goes on such lists. Surely you must make some similar sort of domestic duty roster at times. The lock on that door. The oil on that hinge. Put up that bird house, Burton, the one you bought last winter.

But to get back to the Christmas shopping. (You see what I mean? Even on paper I am endlessly pestered by distractions.)

Let us say that I shall arise on the very morrow with the singleminded, iron-willed purpose of getting started on my Christmas shopping (which I have been planning all fall to do early).

Perhaps (I think on the day before) I can even finish my Christmas shopping tomorrow. Just wade right into it. No shilly-shallying. Just check my list, make up my mind, go out and get what I want, take it home. I can imagine with what triumph I shall brush my hands together at the end of my swift, assured shopping tour and say: "Well, that's that!"

I am the same way when I make those lists on the night before. I confidently put in more stuff than a handful of picked men could accomplish in three days.

That is because tomorrow has one wondrous, magical quality. Tomorrow is elastic. Tomorrow – or at least my tomorrow – is the most flexible thing since the invention of guttapercha and the most all-containing object since the whalebone corset.

But we loiter. Let us get on to the morning of my Christmas shopping day. I begin briskly enough. But I slow down for breakfast because this is the first meal

Christmas in My Bones

of the day and should be enjoyed. It should be considered and consumed, not grabbed and gulped. Undue haste at this point is undermining our country. It is racking our citizenry with commuter's palsy, nervous fits, gastritis and distemper.

Breakfast should be tasted, respected and relished.

Delays come because I take half-a-dozen telephone calls during breakfast. A few I also make because I happen to think that I should have made them yesterday.

Eventually I do finish, wipe my chin, put on my muffler and coat and go downtown. I still have several hours. Buckle down, now, Burton, you can do it.

But I should go to the Post Office first. No telling what I may get in the mail. And in the lobby I meet somebody I haven't seen in quite a while. Not since yesterday anyway. We talk. After all it doesn't take long to pass a few civil words with a friend. Out on the street again I pass a few more civil words with a few more friends.

Eventually I am in a store. Many other people are there and I know most of them. I don't like to just brush rudely past someone I know without so much as a howdy-do. I find time to check my list and look at the goods displayed among the cheery tinsel and the bright baubles. I see something that is almost what I want. Maybe. Well, maybe not quite.

There's something. Say, that's very nice. For Martha Jane. Well, she has something like it. Or almost like it. Near enough. Still.... Yes. No. Perhaps. Well, I'll look around some more. More stores. More people. More indecision.

W.C. "Mutt" Burton

I'm out again. I look up; one should pause to enjoy the color of the winter day. What lovely color in the sky! And what is making those lovely colors? The sun going down, that's what.

You know something? Most of us wind up too many days feeling like somebody who has been pushed too fast in a cafeteria line.

Christmas Present and Past

I am writing this late Christmas night. The streets of Reidsville have been blessedly quiet this day. As I looked about the town this Christmas Day, my vision, under the influence of intoxicating memory, was filled not only with what I saw, but what I recalled. The simplest view was a paste-up, a montage of many things taken from some four score other Christmas Days I have seen in this town and superimposed on this day.

In the parking lot of a food store, which obligingly kept its doors open all Christmas Day for the benefit of people who just forgot one or two little things in the Christmas Eve bustle, I saw a little boy with a pleased look on his face, the remnants of the morning's excitement still traced about his eyes, playing with a toy gun. Immediately, I saw playing with him on that lawn of pavement a multitude of little boys who have

Christmas in My Bones

run out doors on Christmas Day with a new toy gun and a happy shout.

That number would include myself and I can recall the mysteriously satisfying sound of the cork stopper on a new popgun as clearly as if that echo had not died away three quarters of a century ago. (I cannot share the alarms of the child psychologists, real or phony analysts, who run a fever over the fascination a toy weapon holds for a small boy. Such devices never developed any strains of hostility toward anybody in me. All I ever got out of a toy gun, pistol or cannon was pure and happy fun.)

Another youngster was riding south on traffic-teeming Scales Street on a new bicycle, one of those rangy-looking, awkward seeming style bikes that looks like it was patterned after a long-horn steer. The boy pedaled along in bumptious pride of his shiny new vehicle, looking over his shoulder part of the time and weaving perilously close to the main path of the cars which made two counter-flowing streams of danger.

Other bicycle Christmases came to mind, my own and those of many chums and companions. In years that have vanished, a bicycle Christmas was a very special Christmas, a super-Santa Christmas, a big time in a boy's life. The bikes were brought into the streets in the earliest light of winter dawns for wobbly first try-outs by the novice and for "no-hands" derring-do by the boy whose Christmas bike was a new one but not his first one.

We took over the block and if even one car chugged along before noon we cleared the streets blocks ahead of the trespasser and waited until it had

Christmas in My Bones

run out doors on Christmas Day with a new toy gun and a happy shout.

That number would include myself and I can recall the mysteriously satisfying sound of the cork stopper on a new popgun as clearly as if that echo had not died away three quarters of a century ago. (I cannot share the alarms of the child psychologists, real or phony analysts, who run a fever over the fascination a toy weapon holds for a small boy. Such devices never developed any strains of hostility toward anybody in me. All I ever got out of a toy gun, pistol or cannon was pure and happy fun.)

Another youngster was riding south on traffic-teeming Scales Street on a new bicycle, one of those rangy-looking, awkward seeming style bikes that looks like it was patterned after a long-horn steer. The boy pedaled along in bumptious pride of his shiny new vehicle, looking over his shoulder part of the time and weaving perilously close to the main path of the cars which made two counter-flowing streams of danger.

Other bicycle Christmases came to mind, my own and those of many chums and companions. In years that have vanished, a bicycle Christmas was a very special Christmas, a super-Santa Christmas, a big time in a boy's life. The bikes were brought into the streets in the earliest light of winter dawns for wobbly first try-outs by the novice and for "no-hands" derring-do by the boy whose Christmas bike was a new one but not his first one.

We took over the block and if even one car chugged along before noon we cleared the streets blocks ahead of the trespasser and waited until it had

W.C. "Mutt" Burton

Houses shut tight against the night
Crack open in the morning sun
And crystal light,
And let the people out
To move about,
To start the new day's work.
Faces grow rosier than the east.
Breath rolls out in smoky vapors
And the smell of hot, gulped coffee –
As incense to the altar of the East.

Down the block an automobile,
Icy pile on polished steel,
Coughs against the winter's grip,
Rips the silence among the houses
Along the street.
It roars to limber up its sluggish pistons
To warm its oily blood
And go growling and
Snarling away down town,
Spitting fumes from the deepest pits
Of Texas, Oklahoma and Pennsylvania,
And belching smoke, a dyspeptic dragon,
Eager to reach the field of conflict
And fight for a parking space.

It is a winter day being born,
In some ways like any winter day
Opening up for business,
Setting up shop,
Doing its regular job.

Christmas in My Bones

But it is not just any winter day
Or just any old time
In the winter season.
One knows.
One knows.
One can tell –
Or, anyway, any child can tell,
No matter how young or old.

There is in this air a special lightness
And in this light a special brightness,
And in the clearness laughter newly tuned.
There is a quiet singing in this day.

High noon with high heart
Comes to split the day apart
And point the shadows north.
Time, suspended, hangs in even lustre,
Serene and clean against the trees and walls,
And, moving westward with the sun,
Brings afternoon and dusk – and day is done.
It moves too fast? You'd have it stay?
It goes to start another day.

Watch the day,
Watch the night.
Don't let them go unseen.
Look at the light,
Walk with it across a field
Or see it falling through a window,
Changing, forming visions, colors,

W.C. "Mutt" Burton

gone on before returning to our rightful domination of the thoroughfare. Watching this youngster on this Christmas Day pumping his way along a perilous path I reflected that my day in the saddle of a trusty Ivor Johnson (not infrequently referred to in all seriousness as "Ivory Johnson") was certainly a much better one for bike riders.

Today's traffic makes no provision for the bike. With the Detroit deluge surging along every highway and city street some cities have begun providing special bicycle lanes, much as city park systems provide bridal paths for the regrettably obsolete horse and admirably obstinate rider.

These were some haphazard thoughts on Christmas Day. Through every wreathed window, in every tree-spangled room I passed, on every sidewalk and street corner and yard, I found fragments of past Christmas Days without ever once losing, in that oddly cherished melancholy, the rich awareness of this one.

Mo Christmas

Nothing refreshes the spirit of Christmas in old, tired bones more than children at Christmas time. The tingle in their eyes and the growing excitement in their voices as the season approaches can warm the heart of even the most dour Scrooge.

One year at our house – can it really have been nearly twenty years ago now? – we had what we dubbed to be "Mo" Christmas. I am not writing with a Southern accent. "Mo" is our granddaughter and she is called that because her middle name is Morehead. When she was younger and wished to be formal about it she referred to herself as "Anna Mo."

This was "Mo's" biggest Christmas, not because she received more gifts than on previous Christmases, but because she was at exactly the right age for Christmas to begin working its wonderful magic to her. She was not quite half-past-three. To be exact, she was three years, four months and 20 days old on Christmas Day.

"Mo" had liked Christmas all along, of course, but the realization of the jolly time had reached a new flowering with her present age. She had been looking forward to it ever since the first leaf fell. She grew excited at the mere picture of a Christmas tree, and when we put up our tree she was beside herself with joy.

It was, I think, the most beautiful Christmas tree I ever saw, a deep green, fully foliaged, fresh-as-mint tree from Howard Briggs, but you know about that.

"Mo" would gaze at the tree, run up to it, touch the soft, long needles lightly with her forehead and laugh with delight because "it 'ickles." (She was not yet in complete command of all consonants.) When it was decorated with lights, fat tinsel garlands, gold and silver balls and the fantasy pieces, such as small gingerbread men and thin wooden snowflakes from Germany, she was entirely entranced. Now and then she would go to the tree and kiss it. Her eyes shone brighter than the tree lights and all the Christmas candles put together.

For many days before the season was visible over the horizon, we read, again and again, to her, a variety of her books, especially those touching upon the hovering Yuletide. Often she would have the same story repeated two or three times. She had a beautifully illustrated book containing the words of the old carol, "The Twelve Days of Christmas."

I don't know how many times I read "Mo" that

Christmas in My Bones

book. I even sang it in a faltering, muted and limited baritone. She knew it, too, not from my raspy renditions, but because she often went to sleep at night (and for her afternoon nap) while programs of Christmas hymns and carols were going softly on the record player. She liked to drift off into Christmas dreams with Good King Wenceslas or the Herald Angels. And a partridge in a pear tree.

Neither King Wenceslas nor the angels could sing "The Twelve Days of Christmas" better than "Mo." The sequence of days and gifts was sometimes a little irregular and some or the consonants were missing, but her soft and lovely treble was remarkably faithful to the melody and completely faithful to the spirit.

"Mo" spoke of Santa Claus a great deal, of course, and with obvious affection. She was pretty well equipped with images of the jolly old elf and was constantly confronted with his picture in books, magazines and on cards. The name Santa Claus did not stick with her as much as did his other best-known name, Saint Nick. In "Mo-ese" it came out approximately as "Haint Nick," with the two words run together, rendered more nearly as "Heynick." We understood her, and that is the use of language.

Several times a day "Mo" would demonstrate her affection for "Heynick" by kissing his picture or holding it against her cheek. Other images, such as two inflatable Santas (one in the form of a chair so that, in effect, she sits in Santa's lap) received such favors from time to time. She liked the old boy's white whiskers and red suit and fur-rimmed cap, which she referred to as a "Heynickhat."

The religious meaning of Christmas, the Holy Season, had been explained to her and she was entranced by our creche. Her approach to these symbols was, as it should be, informal, intimate and sweetly personal. She sometimes would take the "Baby Jee-shuss" from his manager cradle and cuddle Him after her fashion. Eventually we bought "Mo" her own set of creche figurines, and she would spend a good deal of time rearranging assorted wise men, shepherds, sheep, angels and members of the Holy Family. At night she slept with the cradled "Baby Jee-shuss" by her pillow.

On the morning of Christmas Day, "Mo" was in a transport of joy. More important to her, however, was the fact that she was in a little red wagon. That was one of the items high on her most-wanted list. Other things to which she gave special priority were a "cook'tove," a "choo-choo-'rain" and "P'ay-Doh." "P'ay-Doh" is a modeling compound which comes in several different colors and a single sickly sweet odor which I abhor, but which "Mo" much admired. "Don' it 'mell good?" she asked with enthusiasm. I weakly agreed. She would not understand olfactory senses unable to appreciate the perfume of "P'ay-Doh."

She received all of those priority items and many more besides, including dresses, more books, records, puzzles, dolls and a tea set, essential for holiday entertaining. She played hostess to her mother, her grandmother, me, Abigail, Pickwick, Snodgrass and Sam Weller.

A Dickens devotee at the age of three, "Mo" was fascinated with the names of those last three especially. She received a green panda bear and promptly

Christmas in My Bones

named it Sam Weller. Pickwick and Snodgrass, along with the non-Dickens Abigail, were entertained at tea only in her imagination. Abigail was an imaginary character of "Mo" manufacture. She was apparently very small and was sometimes carried about in one of "Mo's" pockets. She was also invisible to all – except "Mo," who frequently talked to and about her earnestly and at length.

The cook stove, I might add, was an especially charming toy. It was a cast iron replica in miniature of the old Crescent range, which burned either wood or coal. It had removable stove lids, a tiny stove key, cast iron kettle, frying pan, coal scuttle and shovel. The iron oven door would swing open and "Mo" "cooked" everything in that oven from innumerable concoctions plucked from the cupboard of make believe to a vast variety of "P'ay-Doh" recipes, all of which she pretended to consume with a smacking of lips. She generously shared them with the rest of us as well – generously and insistently.

I forgot to say that one of the first things "Mo" did with her "P'ay-Doh" was blend the red and blue. This was done, not without needed and kneading assistance from her grandmother and me, because "Mo" was intensely fond of the color purple. "I yike burple," she said emphatically, whenever she saw anything of that hue. There was a color-diagram on the package showing how to make "burple P'ay-Doh."

She "yikes" Christmas certainly, pronouncing the holiday almost exactly like "isthmus" ("of Suez"). "Mo" also "yikes" a log fire. "Make a hot," she urged me and loved to crumple newspapers for the purpose.

(In this we were both watchful and warning.) In the afternoon of Christmas Day, "Mo" sometimes sat in her hand-made Carolyn rocker, made by the Woody brothers of Spruce Pine in the mountains of North Carolina, (another of her gifts), and gazed reflectively into the log fire which lighted her sweet face with mystery. Clearly she was meditating on the beauty of Christmas.

She loved the Herrnhut Stars (Moravian) which lighted two of our windows and greeted them daily. "Morning, Herrnhut 'ar," she chimed, managing the "Herrnhut" perfectly but ignoring the "st" in "star." She liked also, at times, to wear a Santa Claus cap ("Heynickhat") which she found in my oddly miscellaneous wardrobe.

She was entranced by the tree. From time to time she would sit almost under it, looking up at its bedecked brilliance, her lovely little face more radiant than all its lights and baubles. She was the very spirit of the season, Christmas present, Christmases now past and Christmases yet to come.

The Christmas Feeling

Slide the trombone gently, sweetly,
Keep the brasses down discreetly.
Muffle drums to soft and mellow,
Here's a solo for the cello.
Agitate the tambourine,
Celebrate this Christmas scene.
What makes up the world's wild song
As Yuletide shoppers move in throng?
Hear the small frost-bitten band
Tooting bravely to the land
Carols old but ever new,
Wrapped in coats and capes of blue.
Faces reddened by the cold
They tell the tidings angels told.
"Help the needy," hand-bells ring,
In the churches choirs sing

W.C. "Mutt" Burton

"Oh, little town of Bethlehem."
From streets the gathering noises stem,
Sounds of feet that shuffle fast,
Sounds of autos moving past,
Sounds of opening, closing doors
As mobs move in and out of stores;
Voices in excited babble
Of gift-seekers' ceaseless gabble.
A music box's tinkling air
Concealed within a teddy bear;
Children's voices shout in glee –
And merrily impatient key.
The chimes in lofty towers mingle
With the cash drawer's nervous jingle.

What makes up the Christmas sight?
Candles glowing in the night
Whose onyx sky and piercing star
Seem nearer than the candles are;
Christmas trees in gaudy glitter,
Floors, beds, tables in gay litter;
Holly green and mistletoe
And the firelight's warming glow;
Radiance on family faces,
Parcels cached in secret places.
Christmas cards in bright array
From friends next door and far away;
Lengthy lists and looming debt
And Dickens on the TV set.
What makes up the Christmas smells?
All the things the market sells;

Christmas in My Bones

Winter air with tang of wine,
Fragrance of the fir and pine,
Incense of the candle wick,
Cakes with icing piled on thick;
A thousand other small perfumes
That fill the decorated rooms.

What makes up the Christmas feeling?
Tasks that set our heads to reeling,
Weariness of nerve and bone –
But not these things and these alone
A sweet excitement deep inside,
Full thanks that home and friends abide,
That people sing and children play
In celebration of this Day;
For gifts in token, loving lines;
Assurance that The Star still shines.
And deeper still a peaceful glow
As quiet as the silent snow,
A knowing hope, a sense of cheer
To carry through another year.
And so good friends, to all I send
The best of wishes without end,
God keep us all from harm and fear,
Merry Christmas, glad New Year.

Christmas in Old Salem

However frequently and futilely we may repeat the familiar poetic prayer of Elizabeth Allen, "Backward, turn backward, O Time, in your flight," we who are blessed to live in North Carolina do have a practical, simple and delightful way of stepping back into time. Anyone who is not already familiar with the Old Salem Restoration in Winston-Salem and its engaging features should correct this deficiency with as little delay as possible.

I cannot imagine any person of sense and sensibility failing to find it delightful. And as an avenue to Christmas the Moravian candle teas and the Christmas Eve lovefeasts and candle services are unsurpassed in their beauty and effectiveness, enjoyed as they are in an atmosphere which has been mellowing for 200 years.

Christmas in My Bones

Because of my own well-laden Christmas schedule I am never able to spare even a part of a Christmas Eve away from home, so I have never attended the lovefeasts; our daughters have and their reports are glowing. The candle teas, held the first two weekends in December, I have attended and can report on.

I might add that at any season whatever Old Salem exerts such a charm upon the visitor that only one objection rises to be considered. You may want never again to leave it.

Those hardy Christian Protestants, who fled Moravia (now a part of Czechoslovakia) to the New World in 1735 and settled their 100,000-acre tract called Wachovia in North Carolina in 1753, were strong in faith and spirit. They were hard-working, thrifty and resourceful and they were also lovers of music and fine craftsmanship. These qualities are everywhere evident in enchanting Old Salem.

The candle teas are held in the Brother's House across from Salem Square. Built in 1769 and lovingly restored, its front door is the portal for re-entry into its original century. Visitors who come for the candle teas are collected in groups in the warm reception hall and then moved into an anteroom where tenants of the house once left their coats and hats to move directly into the little chapel of the house for evening worship before supper. The rustic wooden pegs are there in rows, high against the rough plastered wall. One almost sees the heavy homespun garments hanging there, well worn and still warm from the strong bodies gone these 200 years. Once young Moravian men came to live, learn piety and a trade.

Christmas in My Bones

Through the old chapel door sift the sounds of caroling and the sweet reeds of an ancient organ. A lady in the Moravian costume of the 1700s provides footnotes which both fill out and stir the imagination.

Thus guided and informed, one moves through the corridors and rooms, down the stairways and under the great beams of the building, every wall and timber breathing the strength and peace of a time long past. It gets into one's bones. The present yields to the past and one is given at least a temporary lease on complete serenity.

From the anteroom each party moves into the chapel itself. There seated on the simple benches before the gleaming chief ornament of the chapel, the 170-year-old Tannenberg organ, one joins in the caroling and hears such transporting melodies as the traditional Moravian Christmas hymn, "Morning Star." The organist plays and speaks with gentle humor and persuasion. (A songsheet and brochure are received when one comes in the building.)

Here, too, the Hussite Bell Choir performs, four young boys who ring out with handbells the seasonal airs in such goldenthroated tones that all the Christmas times forever seem embraced in their melodic joy.

After the music, one moves into a downstairs chamber where the Moravian Christmas candles are being made and the honeyed incense of melting beeswax fills the air, tinctured with the scent of hot coffee and sugarcake delectably hinting the treat in the adjoining kitchen. The freshly made candles may be bought there so that one may fill one's own home with this most pertinent and pungent of Christmas odors.

W.C. "Mutt" Burton

Then into the old, brickovened kitchen with its floor of square paving bricks and its delicious refreshment served from wooden trays by bonneted women. From the kitchen the party moves on to view an astonishingly realistic scale model of the early village of Salem, a view that visiting angels might have seen, its rooftops white and its lighted windows slanting their rays across the snow.

Finally there is the viewing of the "putz" the figurines and miniature topography representing the people and places of that first Christmas in Bethlehem. The making of such scenes, with painstaking art, is a Moravian custom. Special lighting, music and a reading of the Christmas story from the Bible dramatize the quaintly captivating scenes.

Moving out again under the starry Christmas sky, one is apt to recall the meaning of the word "salem," and to murmur on one's wintry breath "Salem on earth, good will to men."

Christmas Memories

There are those who hold fast to the belief that the Star in the East, borne by angels, is something that happened in fact. There are others who see it as myth. To most of us it is something that shines in our hearts and heritage with the lustre of reality and truth. It is the symbol and annunciation of Christmas and there is no other season, no festival in all of Christendom even remotely like it.

For whatever reason, the stars of Christmas are, to me, like no other stars of the year. They are clearer, brighter. They twinkle more. They have a happier glow. I have no doubt that science can offer perfectly valid reasons for these manifestations, but I shall continue to believe there is a special shine to the Yuletide, a poetry beyond the reach of reason. On a clear day too, there is a particular cheeriness in the light, and cloudy days at Christmastide have a crystalline quality like no other cloudy days.

You may tell me, if you like, that all this happens inside me, in my mind, my heart, my imagination. This may be true. But then nothing really lives that does not live in the mind, heart and imagination.

I do not consciously remember my first Christmas: It occurred just over a month after I was born. Experts in matters mental say, however, that all such items are tucked away in the little gray cells which are in charge of the unconscious, a sort of holding pattern of memory. I think that is true. Certainly every Christmas comes fully equipped with memories and fragments of memories of all our Christmases that have gone before. They are bright greetings from the past, countless invaluable extra Christmas gifts.

Even though I cannot remember my first Christmas, at least not with any image clarity, and I'm not too clear about my second for that matter, I can say in truth that I have always loved Christmas. Very likely I didn't make much of a to-do about anything that first December but I'd be willing to wager I didn't utter a single "Bah! Humbug!" I'm pretty sure I cooed and gurgled right joyously about my second Christmas. I may have even said a happy word or two, but it wouldn't sound like much today in the unlikely event that I could recall it. You had to be there.

Each person must surely have Christmas memories of different shapes and shadings. Certain particular ones come back to me with great regularity every year, usually spliced in with a few that may have dropped out a few years. The regular ones are like

Christmas in My Bones

favorite re-runs. As a child I would often get so excited over the approach of Christmas that I could hardly eat or sleep. That was something of a distraction but there was pleasure in it too.

Among the vast store of Christmas memories which I have gathered over the turning years, some were painful at the time, tortuous in their way, but gilded and burnished by time. They shine now among the most lustrous of things recalled.

There was, for instance, a Christmas many years ago (but the memory is immediate and vivid) when the Christmas tree was placed in the room where I slept, for reasons not included in the recall. I had been building up inside myself for the glorious season for weeks. The tension had become a sweet agony; nevertheless it was true tension and very real agony.

That softly shining, eerily twinkling tree held me hypnotized, sleepless, tense with eagerness for the first faint streak of day. In that taut anticipation of the morning and its unbelievable treasures I lay there while time lagged, dragged, stood stock still. I would not close my eyes or take them from the splendor and the promise of that tree. In a state of wide-awake Christmas catatonia I remained all night long. Or so it seemed.

It was not, as it might appear, a longing for material treasures. I expected and always got things I liked – or liked the things I got – but my gifts were always modest in money costs. My father ran a neighborhood grocery store, which fed us, clothed us, kept us sheltered and warm; but few and simple were the so-called luxuries. Looking back I am glad that was so.

No, it was my whole excited, Christmas-saturated state of mind. I did not think of what I was going to get as Christmas gifts. I did not consider what, as such would bear my name under that now ghostly-seeming tree. It was, in fact, everything about Christmas – the songs, the old, old beloved stories and images, the lighted candles and the lighted windows of churches and homes, the bright baubles on the evergreen.

I remember exactly how that tree looked. There must have been a bright moon in the winter sky because a soft, silvery light fell through the big window opposite the tree, bathing it with a luminous, shadowless imagery that seemed to come from inside the tree itself. Every dripping foil tinsel and every glistening ball and bauble picked up what seemed a supernatural glow. It held me in a state of hypnotic expectation. I began to feel as if I were floating in a silver haze.

Somewhere along in the very smallest of hours I did drop into unconsciousness and of course, the morning of Christmas Day which had been an eternity coming, did come. And I got my gifts. And liked them. I remember some of the things I got only because of the way the late afternoon came to a suddenly slack and let-down close. I remember three of them clearly. There was a shiny, colored, enameled tin drum. There was a pocket knife that was a cherished item. There was a book – there always was and always will be a book. Two or three other things, which I do not recall.

It was a cold Christmas Day, a bright day but with a curious flat light which seemed to mirror the mood I

Christmas in My Bones

carried all day, after the first excitement of surprises; the greatest surprise being that Christmas Day actually did arrive, and the opening of presents.

In the late afternoon, a cold, bleached sun lowered itself into a cold, bleak sky. Not even the red rim of the West could warm it. I could not hold out any longer. In a last hollow effort to fortify my spirits, to salvage some cheer from the day I had looked forward to so terribly, I gathered my gifts, piled them on or about the tin drum, and broke into sobbing surrender.

My mother and father comforted me; showed me understanding and smiling support. I achieved some sense of proportion some tincture of philosophy.

And from that day to this I have enjoyed every minute of Christmas, the time approaching Christmas Day and the 12 days of Christmas that follow it, without despair or disappointment.

I am not sorry that such Yule extremes no longer seize me but I'm glad I remember them. I'm glad, too, that I still do feel much of the excited delight that I felt when somewhat younger on every threshold of Christmas and throughout its 12 days. I do not get in such a fever of fixing nowadays. I have no traffic with tissue and tinsel any longer. I do not wrap gifts, but I'm glad that others do. Long ago, I gladly turned over the adorning and lighting of the tree to Martha. She then passed it to Martha Jane and Anna B. Granddaughter "Mo" has taken over the task more recently. Apart from mounting the tree in its holder and keeping it well watered, the extent of my involvement is to place my chair, by custom, close by it and bask in its green and gleam.

W.C. "Mutt" Burton

The grandchildren, of course, the daughters and their husbands are bountiful sources of continuing Christmas recollections in our family. There was the time, for instance, when "Mo" yearned to sleep the night through under the magical canopy of our Christmas tree. (Takes after her grandfather, I always say.) We made a pallet for her under the tree and there she spent the night, her face a radiance of joy.

There was grandson Jason's gleeful countenance on Christmas Morning when he got his computer.

More eventful, though much like those cases, was Martha Jane's rocking horse Christmas, when a shipping error was not discovered until nearly two o'clock Christmas morning. I went downtown and with the aid of a police officer equipped with the spirit of the season and a powerful flashlight, managed to find a beautiful rocking horse in a store. The store manager, just getting to bed after an exhausting day but being filled with that same spirit, dressed and came back downtown. Martha Jane had a beaming Christmas morning. At later ages, Anna B., "Mo" and Jason all went dashing on that same steed, now outgrown but still not spavined.

Another lasting image in my heart is that memorable, and momentarily distressing, Christmas morning when Anna B., sitting in a sea of discarded wrappings, amid her gifts, suddenly burst into tears. A few seconds later she came out with the reason for the tearful flow and it wasn't unhappiness at all. "It's so beautiful!" she said. And so it is and always should be.

Among a myriad of other memories is the view of my father's back as he pulled one of our first Christ-

Christmas in My Bones

mas trees along, while I followed his steps through the woods on a sunny day. And my mother getting out the boxes of decorations while one of her indispensable and incomparable chocolate layer cakes baked in the oven of the old-fashioned Majestic range in the kitchen, the incense of the cocoa bean flavoring the entire house. And Martha, with wifely ingenuity, defying logic by making a Christmas gift for me which I didn't even know I wanted but discovered I certainly did. Some are, after many years and much use, still giving pleasure.

The most aromatic of my Christmas memories is the fragrant recollection of my father's grocery store in the days approaching merry season. The pot-bellied stove was kept fired up to a point which kept its gray iron sides a rosy red from morning until night. A sociable circle of customers and friends was ringed around it almost permanently, their cheeks tingling pleasantly with its radiant warmth.

Trade always picked up just before Christmas. There was an air of excitement and bustle about it. It was more than just increased business. The orders were different, more festive than usual. People were buying more good things to eat.

They bought fat brown coconuts in their bearded shells. If they were genuinely gifted confectioners of coconut cake, as, say, Bertha McCallum Blank was, they scorned the cans of "prepared coconut." They labored lovingly over the true fruit.

The shell had to be punctured in one of its "eyes" so the milk could be drained from it and saved for the ultimate mix. Then the shell was broken open, sometimes a task requiring a surprising amount of strength. The heavenly white meat was pried out in chunks, the brown inner rind peeled off, and the chunks of meat grated by hand. After this, the sugar and flour and eggs and butter could be brought into play, the oven made ready and the savory artistry begun. The aroma in the kitchen became maddening and the snowy, fluffy masterpiece that emerged from this culinary alchemy was delicious beyond the power of language. It was poetry out of a cake pan.

I have eaten many a slice of excellent coconut cake in my day, but Bertha Blank's coconut cake is treasured by the taste buds of my memory. The golden layers were moist with the rich coconut milk and the filling and frosting were thick and creamy, mostly made of the grated meat and without a single stringy piece or tough fibre. It dissolved on the tongue like a benediction and rested on the tummy like a caress.

I guess I shouldn't have mentioned the coconuts (my father, as I recall, handled them only at Christmas time). I got carried away there, but that cake was worth the space.

As I was saying, people bought goodies. Crystallized fruit for fruit cakes. I could rhapsodize further on a white fruit cake with which Bill and Suzie Hutcherson used to provide Martha and me at Christmas. It contained almost no flour, was made of fruit and fresh coconut. But I'd only be punishing myself.

And, of course, they bought oranges and tangerines and almonds and walnuts and pecans and Brazil nuts. There was a brisk trade in Baker's chocolate, too, and a note of happy expectancy in such orders. Fat,

Christmas in My Bones

juicy raisins, sweet grapes cured in the bunch and still clinging to the viny tendrils, were piled in boxes on the counter. At Christmas, we called them "sugar plums" and many a bunch would go in many a holiday bowl. They would rest by the wooden nut bowl with its center island bristling with nut picks and nut crackers, a standard item of Christmas equipment in most homes of my youth. There were also baskets of malagas and scuppernongs.

Since, in those days, every grocer delivered goods ordered to his customer's kitchens, most of those holiday orders came by telephone and were pedaled out to their various destinations by a boy on a bicycle. The hot stove social circle dispatched its business briefly. Its members would take what they ordered home, but only after the comforts of warmth and amiable conversation had been enjoyed at leisure.

Inside the store the atmosphere of business was only peripheral. The gathering was for neighborliness, companionship, snug shelter and a sharing of the holiday mood.

My father, dressed, as usual, in a dark business suit, complete with vest and coat, starched white shirt, stiff collar and black string bow tie, and with a black, center-creased Stetson hat perched firmly on his head (because it was bald and sensitive to chilly currents of air), moved with expert ease among his bins and shelves, filling the orders. And hurrying back to the stove as quickly as possible. His social life was centered around that stove. Although he liked Christmas, he kept an intense and lifelong hatred for cold weather.

W.C. "Mutt" Burton

There were other exciting things about the store at Christmas time. Packages came in from the wholesale mail order firms my father did business with – and some of them were hidden from my sight with obvious and tantalizing haste.

Looking back, I think I liked best the easy friendliness around that rosy stove, and the great supply of fruits and nuts put in stock for the season. My father, aware of the constant temptation, held a hard line on candy, but he shared the general belief that fruits and nuts were entirely health-giving and allowed me free rein among those natural goodies. So, at Christmas especially, I cracked and peeled to my heart's content – and my stomach's limit.

I can still smell, in aromatic memory, the delectable fragrance of my father's store. The wholesome smell of meal and flour and slab bacon, the enticing redolence of fresh-ground coffee and of a great barrel of brown sugar (from which I was permitted to a generous lump often enough) were heightened at Christmas by the spicy orange smell, the piquant scent of tangerines and grapes and "sugar plums," the subtle, but tempting musk of bins of nuts. It was a treat to breathe there.

My father's store was always an agreeable place to be, but in this season of cheer it was particularly pleasant. It smelled and it tasted like Christmas.

The Mysteries of Christmas

Our Christmas tree is still fresh-looking, green and handsome, as I write this. But unlike other times when I have written about our trees – each, of course, the most beautiful ever – this time there is a difference.

The tree has been stripped of its lights and jewelry. The shining glass balls of silver and gold, the red ones, the blue ones, are gone. Like spherical, multicolored mirrors they reflected the many tiny lights on the tree, the other baubles, the green boughs and the scene in the living room, a gaily distorted panorama of holiday decor mingled with day-to-day living which seemed too commonplace for the tree's special splendor.

The glittering decorations have been packed away in the boxes which, in most cases, have contained them for many years. The brilliantly bristling tinsel

W.C. "Mutt" Burton

has been coiled carefully in the boxes marked "Tinsel" with red markers, and little boxes have been put in bigger boxes, each space calculated over Christmases past to hold the contents as neatly as possible.

There is tradition at work here. The mistletoe ring, for instance, must always be placed in the same box, not merely because it fits perfectly but because it is the box for the mistletoe ring. The larger cases, too, have been in use for many years, ever since we moved to Payment Downs.

The two largest boxes, which are two feet long, 13 1/4 inches wide and 14 inches high hold most of the yule jewelry. Though they are identical in size and general structure, their original contents were very different in character. One of them has "EGGS" in large letters on its sides and once held styrofoam cartons of them. Its matching size is labeled "Peerless Gas Fired Logs." Both were chosen for their present use because they are spacious, not too cumbersome and because they were manufactured with hand slots for easier carrying.

Two other cartons, which now hold shimmering tree trophies, were once laden with "knowledge." One contained a set of the *Book of Knowledge* and the other (from the same publisher) a set of the *Grolier Encyclopedia*. These are made of double laps of heavy cardboard and are admirably sturdy.

One of the boxes is a rather fancy affair which formerly contained even fancier California fruit, sent to us many Christmases ago by our then neighbors, the late Mr. and Mrs. W. B. Kiker. Not only does this box serve its purpose as a nifty container of yuletide orna-

ments, but it repeatedly reminds us of the goodies it bore and of the friends who sent them.

There is a wistfulness, a kind of melancholy which has something oddly enjoyable at its heart, in packing away the home embellishments of Christmas. It means the Twelve Days have gone by once again. The preparation and the holiday season which dressed our daily feelings, our emotions and our vision with extra color and a shared excitement and meaning – gone. It is not that goodwill and peace, which have yet to attain their due popularity and practice, or that merriment in the mind and heart should abandon us, but the time that celebrates them is over, as it has been so often before.

So we turn to a year still in infancy, with its four seasons of hope and change, trying to keep the quality of the good things of Christmas until the radiant season comes again, as it always has and always will, but seeking the joy of life in the offerings of winter, spring, summer, fall. And winter and Christmas again.

In a little while, when I have finished writing this, I will take the tree out of its stand (where I have kept it watered with – after trying numerous other methods – one of those rubber syringes with a long tube used to put water in automobile batteries which still require such treatment; they may still be found in some auto supply stores or auto accessory departments of variety stores). Then I will toss the tree out and feel a little pained and a little mean about doing so after it has served us with such grandeur.

I have already taken all the boxes, large and small, upstairs. I will open the doors in the knee wall of my room and put everything under the eaves, where it all

Christmas in My Bones

fits neatly. This includes two large paper Moravian stars which we bought in a shop in Old Salem long ago. One in an upstairs window and one in a downstairs window, they glow from 15-watt bulbs throughout the season and are as good as new. They are given tender care.

When we first got the stars they were in a small box, unassembled. I put them together, but not without frustration, and I vowed never to take them apart, but to store them whole and safely. Here I will eschew modesty and admit to a bit of ingenuity and persistence not always apparent in me. I obtained two very large boxes (they are approximately 24-inch cubes) in which paper towels were shipped to a local supermarket.

Then I went to work with more cardboard, glue, a sharp knife, stapler, tape and paper fasteners. In the bottom center of each box I constructed a truncated open pyramid into which the bottom point of each star fitted. I fastened clothes pins to two small dowels which reached the width of each box. And I made fitted lids for the boxes. With the stars resting in their pyramids, the dowels crossed inside the boxes and the clothes pins clipped to the upper rims of the stars you could almost throw the boxes down a flight of steps with hardly a jiggle inside or a blunted point. I even put soft nylon rope handles on the sides of the boxes.

At times, when I look under the eaves for other things, as I must often do, I look with fleeting affection at the stored adornments of Christmas. Especially in summer, when the sun blazes in a hot sky, thick leaves stand green and still on their branches and shade looks dark and inviting, I rather enjoy a mixture of exotic, nostalgic, anticipatory senses, all at once.

All the old familiar signs and symbols of Christmas stir a warm and happy feeling inside me, no matter how high the mercury outside.

And here I sit writing again about Christmas, also a custom long observed. I have written a great deal about Christmas over the years. I have tried to write something at least a little new each time, a new event, incident, memory-come-to-mind. I have made an honest, earnest effort to make a new approach, find a fresh angle or at least a fairly new note or two in my prose caroling.

I haven't checked back on this, but I know I have not always succeeded. Perhaps I have never wholly achieved what I tried for. Old, dear cherished things have crept into these writings, sliding in sideways as slyly as you please, to be repeated and repeated again, with a slight turn of phrase if I was lucky.

Well, why not? Why dig and labor to find something new to write about Christmas. Christmas is made up of many old things (and I have written that before, too). Christmas is crammed full of tradition. A good thing. Who would want to omit the old songs, the old stories, the old poems, the old customs? Who would want to forget them? An old-fashioned Christmas is the newest kind of Christmas nowadays. And it gets newer every year because the Christmas spirit renews and refreshes it.

It is a simple, even automatic task to write of the standard tokens, the decorations and the customs. These are the traditional inventory, the prop list of

Christmas in My Bones

Christmas. The writer may set them down easily, with facile rhythm and they will evoke the proper mood. This is so because they have been associated in Christmas with other, less tangible qualities.

It is more difficult to tell of the special way the air smells and feels in the crisp out-of-doors of a Christmas morning. It is, perhaps, impossible to describe the particular nature and the particular clarity of the light on a Christmas Day. These and many other subtle, inexplicable phenomena obtain on The Day and, with varying character, on the days leading up to and away from Christmas Day during the full period that the tone of the season may rightly be felt on the earth.

Who can say exactly what there is about the nights of Christmas Season? Yet there is certainly something – some sense and sight about the night – which I have witnessed every year but can not state in full. It is, perhaps, a kind of poetry upon the earth and in the sky.

The old, clear carols invoke its many spells. The church playlets pantomime its mystery and the King James Versions speak the wondrous words of its beginning, but no one tells all about Christmas.

It is something spelled out in the silent heart of every child who has loved Christmas and every man and woman who has, yearly, grown both older and younger by its mark.

Why is a candle brighter at Christmas time? Why is a fire on the hearth warmer, a friend dearer, a family nearer? Why is a book given at Christmas a cheerier companion than the same or another volume in another month? What is the color of the sky at night and what can gauge the radiance of Christmas stars?

I am sure that these things are true and good. I can not answer the questions.

I expect there are no answers and no need for them. For Christmas is a mystery, the brightest, merriest mystery of all time. And mysteries are not made of answers.